The NATURAL TREASURES of CAROLINIAN CANADA

DISCOVERING THE RICH NATURAL DIVERSITY OF ONTARIO'S SOUTHWESTERN HEARTLAND

The Carolinian Canada Coalition

Edited by Lorraine Johnson

LORIMER

James Lorimer & Company Ltd., Publishers

James Lorimer & Company Ltd. acknowledges the support of the Ontario Arts Council. We acknowledge the support of the Government of Canada through the Book Publishing Industry Development Program (BPIDP) for our publishing activities. We acknowledge the support of the Canada Council for the Arts for our publishing program. We acknowledge the support of the Government of Ontario through the Ontario Media Development Corporation's Ontario Book Initiative. The Ontario Arts Council is an agency of the Government of Ontario.

Canada Council   Conseil des Arts
for the Arts   du Canada

ONTARIO ARTS COUNCIL
CONSEIL DES ARTS DE L'ONTARIO

Library and Archives Canada Cataloguing in Publication

The natural treasures of Carolinian Canada : discovering the rich natural diversity of Ontario's Southwestern heartland / by the Carolinian Canada Coalition ; edited by Lorraine Johnson.

Includes bibliographical references and index.
ISBN 978-1-55028-990-9

1. Natural history — Ontario, Southwestern. 2. Biodiversity — Ontario, Southwestern. I. Johnson, Lorraine, 1960- II. Carolinian Canada Coalition

QH106.2.O5N38 2007   508.713   C2007-903499-3

James Lorimer & Company Ltd., Publishers
317 Adelaide Street West, Suite #1002
Toronto, ON M5V 1P9
www.lorimer.ca

This book is printed on 20% pre-consumer waste paper.
Printed and bound in China.

CONTENTS

INTRODUCTION TO THE CAROLINIAN REGION   9
Kevin Kavanagh and Steven Price

PART I THE PLANTS OF CAROLINIAN CANADA   19
Introduction Wasyl Bakowsky
Chapter 1 Forests of Green   23
Kevin Kavanagh and Gregor Beck
Chapter 2 Ontario's Prairie Peninsula   35
Allen Woodliffe
Chapter 3 Wetlands and Their Plants   47
Deborah Metsger

PART II THE ANIMALS OF CAROLINIAN CANADA   61
Introduction Michelle Kanter
Chapter 4 Mammals: From Bats to Badgers   63
Sandy Dobbyn
Chapter 5 Carolinian Birds and the Changing Neighbourhood   73
Jon McCracken
Chapter 6 The Hidden World of Amphibians and Reptiles   87
Michael J. Oldham
Chapter 7 Below the Water's Surface: Fishes and Freshwater Mussels   99
Shawn Staton and Alan Dextrase
Chapter 8 Tiny Treasures: Butterflies and Other Insects   109
Paul Pratt

PART III CARING FOR NATURE ON THE EDGE   121
Introduction Tom Beechey
Chapter 9 Human Footprints in Carolinian Canada   125
Michael Troughton and William DeYoung
Chapter 10 Stewardship in Action   135
Ric Symmes
Postscript Embrace the Past, Help Shape the Future   147
Gordon Nelson with Michelle Kanter

Glossary   149
Carolinian Places to Visit   150
Further Reading and Sources   152
Contributors' Biographies   154
Acknowledgements   156
Index   157
Photography Credits   160

Dedicated to Henry Kock

May 3, 1952 – December 25, 2005

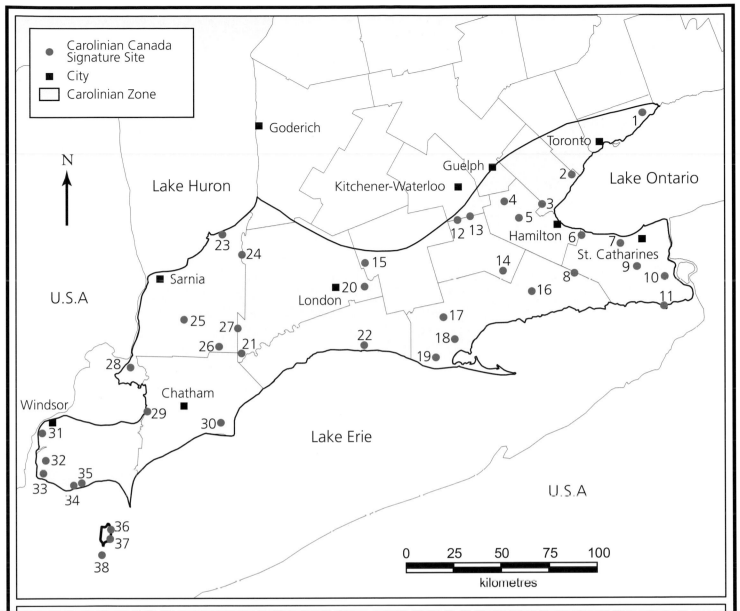

CAROLINIAN CANADA SIGNATURE SITES

Critical unprotected natural areas in the Carolinian Life Zone of Canada identified in 1985

1. Rouge River Valley
2. Iroquois Shoreline Woods
3. Sassafras Woods
4. Beverly Swamp
5. Dundas Valley
6. Grimsby-Winona Escarpment and Beamer Valley
7. Jordon Escarpment Valley
8. Caistor-Canborough Slough Forest
9. Fonthill Sandhill Valley
10. Willoughby Clay Plain
11. Point Abino Peninsula Sandland Forest
12. Sudden Bog

13. Grand River Valley Forests and Spottiswood Lakes
14. Six Nations Forest
15. Embro Upland Forest
16. Oriskany Sandstone and Woodlands
17. Delhi Big Creek Valley
18. St. Williams Dwarf Oak Forest
19. Big Creek Valley-South Walsingham Sand Ridges
20. Dorchester Swamp
21. Skunk's Misery
22. Catfish Creek Slope and Flood Plain Forest
23. Port Franks Wetlands and Forested Dunes
24. Ausable River Valley

25. Plum Creek Upland Woodlots
26. Shetland Kentucky Coffee-tree Woods
27. Sydenham River Corridor
28. Walpole Island First Nation
29. Lake St. Clair Marshes
30. Sinclair's Bush
31. Ojibway Prairie Remnants
32. Canard River Kentucky Coffee-tree Woods
33. Big Creek Marsh
34. Oxley Poison Sumac Swamp
35. Cedar Creek
36. Middle Point Woods
37. Stone Road Alvar
38. Middle Island

Eastern Deciduous Forest

Source:

The Identification Subcommittee of Carolinian Canada, 1985

Ontario Ministry of Natural Resources

PREFACE

Carolinian Canada Coalition

Lush deciduous forests, with abundant ground-covering plants, can be found in the Carolinian region. These woodlands are home to more species of trees than any other region in Canada.

SWEEPING FROM TORONTO TO Grand Bend south to Middle Island in Lake Erie stretches the Carolinian region, an area of biological richness unmatched anywhere else in the country. The trees here have unusual and evocative names: Sassafras, Cucumber Magnolia, Tulip-tree, Pawpaw. These species and others give the region the distinctly southern character for which it is named, after the Carolinas of the southern United States. Pockets of tallgrass prairie and oak savanna echo the great grasslands to the west. Rivers snake through the varied terrain, and coastal and inland wetlands link water with land. Like a bed in an old country farmhouse, the Carolinian landscape sports its own patchwork quilt.

The Carolinian region is tiny, making up only a quarter of a percent of the country's total land area. But it boasts one of Canada's greatest concentrations of vegetation communities and species. Many of these species are living at the northernmost edge of their range, and are found nowhere else in the country. Close to one-third of Canada's rare and endangered plants and animals live in the Carolinian zone. These species depend on the region's distinctive habitats, many of which are also in jeopardy.

A quarter of our nation's population lives in the Carolinian region. Most of our national trade is conducted through border crossings at Windsor, Sarnia, and Fort Erie. Ontario's wine region and some of Canada's best farmland are here as well. The provincial and national economies depend on a prosperous southwestern Ontario. But success comes at a price, and our Carolinian quilt is now quite threadbare.

Since 1984 the Carolinian Canada Coalition has been bringing together organizations, communities, and individuals to conserve the special places and species of the Carolinian life zone. This partnership of more than forty groups has pioneered work in landowner-contact projects, stewardship, research, and education. It has become a powerful voice for protecting the remaining fragments of Carolinian habitat.

The Carolinian Canada Coalition has had many successes over the years. Awareness of this unique region is growing, and research is adding greatly to scientific knowledge. People and communities are rallying to celebrate, steward, and restore the diversity of plants and animals that find a home in the Carolinian zone.

But much still needs to be done. We hope that this book will inspire, encourage, and support the work of conserving the fabric of this unique landscape and of stitching the fragments back together.

Non-profit groups and land trusts have been purchasing properties in Carolinian Canada to protect them in perpetuity. The North American Native Plant Society, for example, owns and stewards Shining Tree Woods, home to endangered species such as Cucumber Magnolia, in Norfolk County.

More often heard than seen, the Eastern Screech Owl can be found in woodlands of various descriptions, and even in urban areas — wherever there are suitable nesting cavities (or nest boxes) available. This small owl is non-migratory, so it requires mice and voles in sufficient numbers year round to keep it fed.

NOTE ON TERMINOLOGY

Throughout this book, there are references to species at risk. More than five hundred rare species and plant communities are documented in Carolinian Canada by the Natural Heritage Information Centre, and considered by many biologists to be at risk, although not yet formally designated as such. In Canada, species at risk are designated for legal protection through a formal process at the federal and provincial levels. The Committee on the Status of Endangered Wildlife in Canada (COSEWIC) is the federal body and the Committee on the Status of Species at Risk in Ontario (COSSARO) is the provincial body that designate species at risk. The following describes what the various designations mean.

Extinct: a species that no longer exists.
Extirpated: a species that no longer exists in the wild in a
    particular region but exists elsewhere.
Endangered: a species that is facing imminent extirpation or
    extinction.
Threatened: a species that is likely to become endangered if
    nothing is done to reverse the factors leading to its
    extirpation or extinction.
Special Concern: a species that may become a threatened or
    endangered species because of a combination of biological
    characteristics and identified threats.

See the Glossary for definitions of other scientific terms used in this book.

INTRODUCTION *to the* CAROLINIAN REGION

Kevin Kavanagh and Steven Price

EARLY AUTUMN LIGHT PEEKS over the eastern horizon along the north shore of Lake Erie, where the air still hangs heavy and warm, thick with moisture. After a calm, clear night, a shallow fog engulfs the nearby wetlands stretching out into Long Point Bay. Only the distant tops of the tallest willows and cottonwoods emerge from the fog like tiny islands, marking the sandy shoreline where the wetlands end and the lake begins. Overhead, dew drips from the dense, emerald forest canopy, tapping like gentle rain on a thick carpet of ferns below.

Well before the sun crests the eastern horizon, the first voice to break the silence is the Swamp Sparrow's, far out in the marsh. In rapid succession follow the ratchet of a Common Yellowthroat, the bugling of Sandhill Cranes, and a building chorus of Red-winged Blackbirds and Common Grackles. In recent weeks their ranks have swollen into the tens of thousands,

The shoreline marshes of Carolinian Canada, particularly those on the shores of Lake Erie, represent some of the most extensive remaining wetlands in the region.

The brilliant red foliage of Staghorn Sumac signals the arrival of autumn.

as they seek nightly refuge in the marsh prior to fall migration. Beneath the leafy forest canopy, quiet darkness lingers, the nightly chorus of katydids and tree crickets now subside in anticipation of the pending dawn. Suddenly, the silence is pierced by the ringing song of a Carolina Wren. In the distant forest depths, calls of a Red-bellied Woodpecker echo and a Gray Treefrog chants. As the marsh fog thins, Great Blue Herons and Great Egrets wade among American Lotus leaves that emerge out of the shallow marsh waters, from which Blanding's Turtles will soon haul themselves out to sun. Night is turning to day, and the abundant creatures of this forest and wetland are stirring to life.

AS ITS NAME SUGGESTS, the Carolinian region of southern Ontario is, in some ways, biologically more aligned with places like North and South Carolina than with the rest of Canada. Summer heat and humidity, as well as — for the most part — moderate winters, further help to define this region. The distinct nature of Carolinian Canada, with its southern affinities, has been recognized and celebrated for decades. Pamphlets about Point Pelee National Park boast that it occupies the southernmost point of mainland Canada, on a latitudinal par with northern California. Tourism slogans along Lake Erie refer to the area as "Canada's South Coast." But the region's climate is caused by more than its southerly location. It is influenced by the adjacent waters of three Great Lakes (in fact four, if the great Lake St. Clair is included). These large bodies of water hold tremendous amounts of latent energy, built up over a long summer season and dissipated through the winter as the waters cool. This process helps both to moderate cold winter temperature and to bolster summer humidity levels. Remarkably, Lake Erie's surface water temperature can reach nearly 27° C by mid-August, a temperature more typical of the Gulf of Mexico.

The Carolinian Canada region stretches west from Toronto's Rouge River valley to the Grand Bend area on Lake Huron, and south to the U.S. border. On an Ontario road map, this is roughly the ribbon of Ontario south of Highways 401 and 402. In contrast to humanity's tendency to demarcate the region by a sharp line, however, nature rarely works with such precision. As a result, the boundaries of Carolinian Canada have been interpreted variously by biologists and foresters, with these variances reflecting different criteria. But when it comes right down to it, there is no hard line in the sand — or clay. As with most natural systems, one does not abruptly step into and out of the Carolinian zone. Instead, if travelling north to south, one gradually moves into locations with a growing abundance and diversity of southern flora and fauna.

Burning Bush, also known by the First Nations name Wahoo, grows in the understorey of woodlands and in moist flood plains. Its showy fruit capsules open to reveal orange-red seeds, which are eaten by birds and small mammals.

While most attempts by biologists to delineate the Carolinian zone have been based on the distribution of plants, especially trees, many species of birds, fish, amphibians, reptiles, invertebrates, and mammals more typical of the south also find a home in this region. And the zone's mild climate has not escaped the attention of others who are also interested in the growth of plants — albeit for different reasons. Farmers relate the boundaries of this region to climatic measures such as crop heat units, growing degree days, and a frost-free season conducive to cultivating wine grapes, tender fruit, tobacco, and even peanuts. Similarly, gardeners may associate the region with the 6a to 7a plant-hardiness zones. No matter what specific measures are used, however, the Carolinian life zone represents one of the most biologically rich areas in Canada, where the natural and cultural mixture of species produces a tapestry of fields, forests, wetlands, prairies, savannas, beaches, and freshwater habitats.

At a finer scale, each area within the region is also highly diverse — a reflection of the many localized microclimates, variable soil types, moisture conditions, and even the quirks of natural and human history. The interactions of these geographical, physical, biological, and social influences over time have resulted in greater or lesser concentrations of species considered to be truly Carolinian in any given locale. In fact, this region, ice-covered for millennia, has undergone, in geological time, a rapid evolution to its current state. With much of the area emerging from beneath a vast ice sheet only twelve thousand years ago, it has seen a succession of ecosystems evolve and shift in response to the changing climate and to the arrival, first, of a succession of native North American cultures, followed by rapid waves of European explorers and settlers.

Swamp forests of the Carolinian region provide habitat for many rare species such as Pumpkin Ash, so named for the swollen base of its trunk. This tree was not known to occur in the region until 1992, when it was discovered by Gerry Waldron in the Devonwood Conservation Area in Windsor.

Today, Carolinian Canada is a region that reflects this dynamic history. Relict populations of northern species remain, mixing with their more recently arrived relatives from the south. Even in the heart of Carolinian Canada, where southern forest icons such as Tulip-tree, Sassafras, Tupelo, and an assortment of oaks and hickories are well established, common boreal species such as Paper Birch and Quaking Aspen persist. Here, Larch and Black Spruce, classic species of northern muskeg, sustain some of their southernmost populations on the continent.

Species with southern affinities edging northward into Canada may represent recent arrivals, as it is likely that ranges for some species are still expanding from the south to occupy available habitats along their northern range edge. Perhaps this is why, despite a long history of exploration of Carolinian Canada's natural areas, even large-statured tree species are still being discovered. For example, the continent's northernmost populations of Ohio Buckeye, Pumpkin Ash, and Swamp Cottonwood have only recently been found, the latter being recorded for the first time in 2002. An even more graphic illustration of this continuing colonization is the emerging evidence of bird species characteristic of more southern latitudes that are rapidly expanding their breeding ranges into Carolinian Canada. Birds such as the Northern Cardinal and Mourning Dove, infrequently observed in southern Ontario only one hundred years ago, have now become common throughout and, in fact, well beyond the region. In the twenty years since the first *Ontario Breeding Bird Atlas* was completed in 1985, new surveys for the second atlas, completed in 2005, show evidence that southern species such as Carolina Wren, Northern Mockingbird, Red-bellied Woodpecker, and Tufted Titmouse are rapidly expanding their ranges into Carolinian Canada.

The influence of early human history is also reflected in the present-day distribution of species. Current populations of valuable food and medicinal plants can reveal locations of historical settlements and prehistoric sacred sites. Ranges of trees with heavy seeds, like Black Walnut and Pawpaw, were almost certainly expanded through early trading cultures, as many of those cultures were themselves migrating northward. Today, wave upon wave of invasive, exotic species from other continents are becoming established here, bringing with them a new threat to the region's native flora and fauna. The drama of the arrivals, interactions, and departures of species continues, as seen in the invasions of Round Goby (fish) and Zebra Mussels in Great Lakes waters, and the extraordinary control measures that government agencies have invoked in recent years to limit the spread of the Emerald Ash Borer and Asian Long-horned Beetle, which threaten the region's forests.

That Carolinian Canada has undergone significant change since European settlement is an understatement. The statistics are staggering. In the little more than two hundred years since European settlement began in earnest, it is estimated that more than 95 percent of wetlands have been drained, approximately 99 percent of the tallgrass prairie has been lost, roughly 90 percent of upland forests have been cleared, and many aquatic systems, including those of the southern Great Lakes themselves, have been enormously disrupted. Even where habitat remains, it often bears the marks of past logging or demonstrates the effects of fragmentation. What was once continuous is now fragmented, remaining natural areas resemble islands of green.

Few parts of Canada — in fact, few parts of North America — have been as extensively and intensively developed as the Carolinian region. First there were sawmills. It may come as a surprise to some that southern Ontario was a major source of lumber in the 1800s. Then, with land clearance and wetland drainage nearly complete by 1900, agriculture took over as the dominant force on the landscape. As wealth and commerce grew, settlements spread inland from the shores of the lakes and along river valleys, prosperous cities and towns blossomed, and urban sprawl began to consume sizable parts of surrounding regions.

From a present-day perspective, early accounts of the wildness of this region take on the qualities of myth. Stories reveal that large carnivores such as Mountain Lion and Black Bear roamed the land, schools of salmon, sturgeon, and paddlefish plied the waters of the Great Lakes, and flocks of Passenger Pigeons, numbering in the millions, would darken the sky as their migratory flocks passed overhead for hours at a time. Quite possibly, a sudden flash of brilliant colour would have revealed the presence of a Carolina Parakeet, or perhaps, on a more subtle note, a Karner Blue butterfly gathering nectar on a patch of prairie wildflowers. Today, most of these creatures are

This spike-rush marsh at Long Point provides outstanding natural habitat for wildlife.

sadly no longer present in Carolinian Canada.

Written barely two hundred years ago, Lady Simcoe's diaries describing her travels through the region in the late 1700s make it clear that what we now call Carolinian Canada was still very much a wilderness frontier. Among her references to the abundant wildlife were stories of rattlesnakes in the Niagara region, including accounts of some measuring over five feet in length that were killed near the camps. These were almost certainly Timber Rattlesnakes, now extirpated from Ontario and rare in many parts of their former range in the United States. After she visited a location near what is now Niagara-on-the-Lake, an entry from her journal, dating from 1792, states, "I did not see any rattlesnakes, though many ladies are afraid to go to Table Rock, as it is said there are many of these snakes near it."

Sought after for food and caught in great abundance as the human population grew and commerce expanded, some species could not sustain the enormous loss of their ranks and became extinct or were extirpated from the region. Fishing fleets on Lake Erie brought in enormous catches. The largest one-day catch ever recorded for a vessel on Lake Erie was thirty-three thousand pounds of herring brought in on a boat from Port Burwell in the early part of the twentieth century. Soon afterwards, the herring fishery collapsed. And this pattern didn't end with herring. Blue Walleye went from being commercially exploited to extinct in a matter of decades. Even if not sought after for the dinner plate, other species such as Piping Plovers could not adapt to the rapid loss in both the quantity and quality of their native habitats, with the result that regional populations were lost from Carolinian Canada. Some, like southern Ontario's breeding population of Bald Eagles or the delicate wildflower Bird's-foot Violet, were luckier, surviving but with their ranks much diminished. Many of these are the species for which today we assign the labels endangered, threatened, or of special concern, and around which recovery efforts are taking place.

Although the growing loss of species and habitats does not appear to have aroused serious concern among settlers until around 1900, earlier accounts exist that questioned the sustainability of both commercial and recreational harvests. Wildlife artist William Pope, for example, reflected in his journal in 1834 about the impacts that duck hunting around Long Point and Turkey Point could be having on staging waterfowl populations:

> *The clouds of ducks at this place are really astonishing, but I am told by old settlers here that they are not so numerous as they were formerly, and that is not to be wondered at as the warfare carried on against them must in some degree lessen their numbers, tho that is small evil compared to the numbers it must cause to quit the place.*

In the end, however, it was the hunting community that advanced some of the region's earliest actions for conservation. In the mid-1800s, wealthy individuals, mostly from the United States, began purchasing wetlands in order to establish private clubs for their members to hunt waterfowl. Much of Long Point, for example, was purchased in this manner in 1866, at a time when development was already beginning to destroy its wilderness character. These exclusive clubs ensured that the extensive shoreline marshes embracing places like Long Point and Turkey Point remained largely free of summer cottages, nor were they drained for market-vegetable production like those on Pelee Island or the marshlands north of Point Pelee.

By 1900, so much forest cover had been removed that the soil was literally blowing away in places like the sand plains of

The American Beech grows into a stately tree with a tall and slender form in dense forests, and takes a more broad and rounded form in open areas. Its most distinctive feature is its smooth, light-grey bark.

Norfolk County. Ontario's first forestry station was established in 1908 at St. Williams to grow tree seedlings that could be planted to slow the loss of soil. Although exotic pine plantations were often the result, today some of these sites are reverting back to more natural forest and oak savanna communities.

Areas with high recreational potential were established as national and provincial parks during the twentieth century. These include many shoreline locales: The Pinery Provincial Park on Lake Huron; Point Pelee National Park, Wheatley, Long Point, Turkey Point, and Selkirk provincial parks along the Lake Erie shoreline; Short Hills Provincial Park in the Niagara region; and Bronte Creek Provincial Park and Rouge Park towards the northern reaches of Carolinian Canada. Additional sites were acquired by Ontario's growing body of Conservation Authorities, especially along riparian corridors. Although some sites were managed for timber production, significant natural areas coming under Conservation Authority ownership included Backus Woods in Norfolk County and the St. John's Conservation Area in Niagara.

Despite the growing collection of protected areas and conservation lands, by the early 1980s there was concern among biologists, both inside and outside of government, that much of the biological variation inherent in Carolinian Canada was not yet represented by these existing sites. In response, a collaborative effort known as the Carolinian Canada Program was launched by government agencies and conservation organizations in the early 1980s to evaluate opportunities to advance new protected areas and other conservation strategies.

By 1984, the Carolinian Canada Program identified thirty-six important unprotected sites, which, when added to the suite of federal, provincial, and local conservation areas and parks, would help to secure for conservation at least one example of all major habitat types in Carolinian Canada. (Two more sites were added subsequently, bringing the total to thirty-eight.) The jumble of issues around their tenure and ownership called for a new and different conservation approach. Government regulation and land purchase would not be sufficient for all thirty-eight sites, nor were they needed everywhere. A program of private stewardship — the encouragement and recognition of landowners' conservation efforts on their own properties — was under rapid development by the University of Guelph, and proved to be a key tool for conservation progress.

Today, these thirty-eight Carolinian Canada Signature Sites demonstrate the remarkable progress of conservation over the past two decades. More than eight hundred hectares of land have

been purchased, raising the total land owned by the public and conservation groups in the thirty-eight sites to nearly six thousand hectares. Some five thousand hectares have been better conserved through voluntary stewardship agreements with nearly five hundred landowners. And through the collaborative efforts of many conservation organizations, additional sites of conservation significance are being secured in similar fashion.

Progress on conserving the Signature Sites came while a new field of science — conservation biology — was emerging and more intensive surveys were taking place to document the fauna and flora of the region. As a result, conservation biologists today have a better understanding of the national, continental, and global significance of natural features in this region. Wetlands along the shorelines of the Great Lakes, for example, still harbour continentally significant flocks of migrating waterfowl. Watersheds like the Sydenham have been discovered to support an incredible diversity of freshwater mussels, many of which are now classified as threatened or endangered due to changes in their habitat and the introduction of invasive, non-native Zebra Mussels. Unusual habitats of thin soils overlying bedrock pavement, known as alvars, support globally significant plant and animal communities in localized sites within Carolinian Canada. Dunes, beaches, and sand-barren communities in the region provide habitat to rare species such as the Eastern Prickly Pear Cactus and Fowler's Toad. And some of the best oak savannas remaining in Canada can be found in the Carolinian zone.

Some of the rarest Carolinian plants and animals are restricted, or nearly restricted, to sandy shores along Lake Erie. At Rondeau Provincial Park, dunes provide habitat for plants adapted to extreme temperatures, drought, and low nutrient levels; vegetation helps stabilize dunes.

The Eastern Prickly Pear Cactus, one of Canada's few native cacti, is a unique plant with fleshy, spine-covered pads and bright yellow flowers. It is found in the wild at Point Pelee National Park, where a boardwalk has been constructed to allow public viewing of this unusual species.

What is shared by all Carolinian species in this region, be they Tulip-trees, Hooded Warblers, or Giant Swallowtail butterflies, is a coincidence of geography. Lined up along their respective northern range edges, the Ontario populations of these southern species are in a prime position to be the forerunners of range expansion northward if confronted by the predicted effects of global warming. Today, this fact alone has the potential to elevate the status of many Carolinian species in Ontario to one of global significance.

EARLY AUTUMN WARMTH HAS intensified as the sun gains altitude over the marsh and forest canopy. Morning voices have now gone quiet for another day. In their place, cicadas are gearing up their buzzing songs, while Monarchs stretch to warm their wings in preparation for another day's flight on their southward journey to Mexico. Although it has changed, there is unquestionably a vibrant rhythm that still plays out daily, seasonally, and across generations here. The nature of change, which has been such a dominant force in Carolinian Canada, both fuels the urgency to do more to conserve these species and these places *and* provides hope that recovery and restoration are possible.

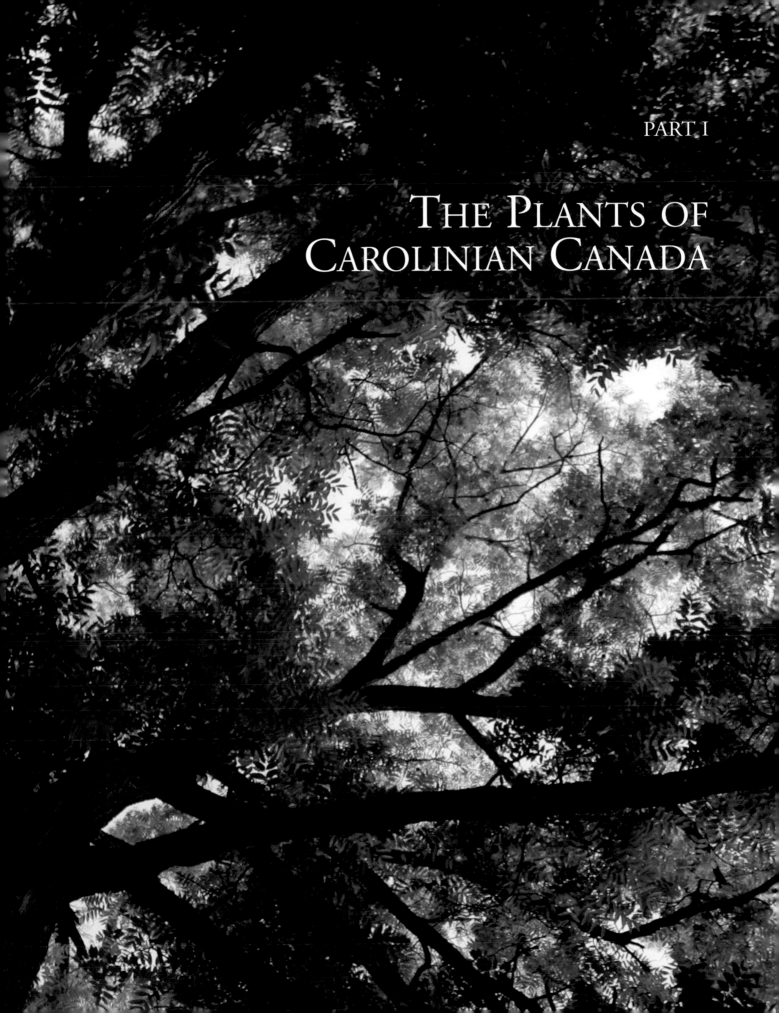

PART I

The Plants of Carolinian Canada

Introduction *to* Part I

Wasyl Bakowsky

"There appears to be one 'boundless continuity' of dark gloomy forest."
— William Pope, aboard a ship on Lake Erie in 1834, describing the dense vegetation of the Carolinian forest

Previous page: The Black Walnut, highly prized as a commercial wood for furniture and cabinetry, is a large tree that can grow to thirty metres. The nuts, enclosed in an aromatic green husk, are eaten by squirrels, rodents, deer, and Red-bellied Woodpeckers, and the leaves are an important food for the Luna moth.

Below: The Carolinian region is best known for its species-rich forests, with southern trees that are found nowhere else in the country.

WHAT POPE SAW as "gloomy" is in fact today recognized as one of the most biologically diverse natural regions in Canada, especially in terms of its lush abundance and rich variety of plant species. Many of the species in the region are found nowhere else in the country.

While many people refer to the Carolinian forest as a single type of forest, there is in fact a great diversity of forest types in this region, reflecting local variations in moisture, soils, and other features. However, despite Pope's assertion, the Carolinian zone has never been a continuous blanket of forest. Open areas of vegetation, such as marshes, fens, and bogs, occur in very wet

sites, for example, though they have been much depleted over the decades. In parts of this region where fires historically swept over the land with some regularity, prairies and savannas developed, often covering hundreds of square kilometres. Remnants of these grasslands still exist, and continue to depend on fire for their survival. Elsewhere, in areas with very shallow soil over limestone bedrock, open alvar vegetation of wildflowers and grasses flourished, and some also remains. The open sandy dunes along the Great Lakes shorelines add yet another specialized habitat and its unique associated species, such as Common Hoptree, to this region.

The plant communities of both forested and open Carolinian habitats are the products of myriad factors interacting over the course of the millennia since Ontario was covered by glaciers. As the glaciers receded from the region, they exposed open lands, which were colonized by plants migrating from unglaciated parts of North America to the west, south, and east. Consequently, the region now supports a mix of plant species with northern, southern, western, eastern, and Great Lakes affinities all finding a place on the Carolinian landscape.

Occupying less than 10 percent of Ontario's landmass, the Carolinian zone is one of the most developed regions of Canada, yet it remains highly diverse. Close to 1,400 of Ontario's more than 2,300 plant species are found in the region, including almost 55 percent of Ontario's provincially rare plant species. This startlingly high percentage of rare plants is in large part due to

The Carolinian zone is one of the most populated areas of Canada. Scattered throughout the region, in places like the Dundas Valley (above), are forested areas that provide habitat for an array of wild plants and animals.

The Small White Lady's-slipper is an endangered orchid found at Walpole Island. Large bees sometimes get trapped in the flower sacs and chew their way out, leaving holes in the flowers.

the scarcity of remaining habitat, which continues to decrease under the pressures of human development.

In addition to the direct impact humans have had on Carolinian vegetation, our remaining pockets of green are being further degraded by invasive exotic species. The plant diversity of upland forests is being reduced through monocultural carpets of Garlic Mustard and thickets of Common Buckthorn and Russian Olive, which displace native species. Undisturbed flood plain forests are now extremely rare, with the majority overrun with the invasive exotics such as Dame's Rocket, Hedge-Parsley, and Moneywort. Wetlands suffer similarly, with Purple Loosestrife and Glossy Buckthorn among the most visible alien invaders.

But all is not lost for the plants of this region. The unique plant communities of Carolinian Canada are now benefiting from new attention. Private landowners who have protected forests, wetlands, and prairies for decades are emerging as conservation leaders. As described in the final chapter of this book, restoration projects, habitat stewardship, and plant-community-based recovery plans are under way, and there is growing awareness and appreciation of this spectacular and diverse region. Perhaps we can find guidance in the words of Anna Jameson, who wrote of the Carolinian forest in 1837, "No one who has a single atom of imagination can travel through these forest roads of Canada without being strongly impressed and excited. Their effect on myself I can hardly describe in words. How savagely, how solemnly wild it was!"

CHAPTER 1

FORESTS *of* GREEN

Kevin Kavanagh and Gregor Beck

One of the most striking characteristics of Carolinian forests is the spring display of woodland wildflowers. White Trilliums (below), Wild Ginger, Hepatica, Spring Beauty, and many other species carpet the ground with colourful blooms.

THE SMOOTH, GREY, ELEPHANTINE trunks of American Beech, centuries old, take on a surreal appearance in the early morning light of a warm and misty spring day. On the forest floor, a lush and diverse assortment of plants is beginning to flower, while sunlight still penetrates the partially leafed-out tree canopy above. Carpets of White Trilliums abound, mixed in places with the large, unfurling leaves of Mayapple and stems of False Solomon's Seal. Scattered throughout are the fast-fading flowers of Trout Lily, Spring Beauty, and Toothwort, which together lead the spring awakening to a new season of growth.

In moister patches on the forest floor, ferns have begun to unfurl new fronds, and horsetails are sending up a myriad of fruiting stems looking for all the world like a collection of randomly scattered miniature clubs. On this fresh spring day, the hints of green do little to foretell what lies ahead in the summer season, when, for several months, this forest will be thoroughly transformed into what can be likened to a northern version of a humid, lush, southern forest, complete with tangled undergrowth and vines stretching into the canopy.

The colour and textural patterns in this carpet of green reflect fine-scale patterns of light and moisture. In wetter spots below the tipped-up mounds of fallen giants, ancient American Beech and Sugar Maple among them, patches of Sensitive Fern are emerging from beneath fallen leaves. Christmas Ferns abound, still sporting a ring of last year's dark-green fronds. On this spring day, the patterns in the forest floor and canopy above reveal the influences of nature's evolutionary forces. Over time, each species has evolved to

Top: Public trails through natural areas and the forests of Carolinian Canada offer rich places for hiking and exploration. Fallen trees on the forest floor provide habitat for many creatures, and, over time, decompose to replenish the soil.

Above: This Pawpaw was found along Little Otter Creek near Vienna, Ontario.

exploit a specific set of light, moisture, and soil conditions, in which it can best compete for a place among its neighbours. The dynamic structure of this forest reflects the forces of nature that worked on past generations of plants.

There are many other species and complexities in forest structure that sneak into the mix. For some of these species, their common names reveal their association with the south, such as Kentucky Coffee-tree, Sassafras, Tupelo, and Pawpaw, to name just a few. For others, such as Cucumber Magnolia, Green Dragon, and Trumpet Creeper, it is the distinctive, showy flowers that suggest more southern origins. Some, like Pin and Shumard Oaks, are more characteristic of the region's extensive clay plains, while others, like Dwarf Chinquapin Oak and Black Oak, are mostly found on well-drained sandy sites. On the forest floor among the carpets of White Trilliums, southern species such as Yellow Mandarin, Broad Beech Fern, Giant Yellow Hyssop, and Rue-anemone compete for space with their more northern relatives.

If there is one forest species emblematic of Carolinian Canada, it is the Tulip-tree. Sporting distinctive leaves shaped like the profile of Dutch tulips, showy orange and green flowers that also resemble tulip blossoms, and trunks that rise like spires to thirty-five or forty metres, Tulip-trees easily pierce the

Top: The cup-shaped flowers of the Tulip-tree, one of the tallest trees of the Carolinian forest, appear in early summer, and are followed by cone-shaped fruit. Its bright green leaves turn glowing yellow in autumn.

Right: A signature tree of the Carolinian region, the Tulip-tree grows quickly in forest openings, towering above other species in the competition for light.

Cucumber Magnolia is a magnificent, showy tree, with abundant yellow-green flowers and distinctive cone-shaped fruit that turns pink or red when ripe in early autumn. It is provincially and federally listed as endangered: there are fewer than 300 naturally occurring Cucumber Magnolias remaining in the wild.

canopies of neighbouring beech and maple. Towering like monstrous heads of broccoli, Tulip-trees spread their foliage and flowers broadly into the sunlight. Only White Pine can match this stature, and in places these two species create a super-canopy of forest giants. One of only two species worldwide representing the genus *Liriodendron* of the Magnolia family, Tulip-trees have evolved to this height in order to maintain their foliage in full sun throughout their life cycle from seedling to maturity — a cycle that can often be as long as two hundred to three hundred years or more. The species produces winged seeds that get well distributed by wind in the vicinity of the parent tree to increase the probability that some may fall in a nearby forest gap — an opening in the canopy created by large neighbouring trees that have succumbed to wind or old age. In such gaps, sunlight finds the forest floor and provides the energy necessary for a small Tulip-tree seedling to grow quickly. If conditions are favourable, a vigorous sapling can grow at the rate of one metre per year. Within thirty years, the young tree can match its canopy competitors in height, and soon thereafter can rise above them. There its branches can be held in abundant light, further improving its chances at longevity.

Tulip-trees need to grow quickly in these large, bright openings, since there are no shortages of competitors jockeying for sunlight. While Tulip-trees require good light from the moment their seeds germinate, other trees, such as American Beech, Sugar Maple, and Eastern Hemlock, are "shade tolerant." These species have a different strategy for recruiting new individuals into the forest. As seedlings, they are able to survive in the deep shade of the forest canopy for years, growing very slowly, waiting for a gap to open above them. If one does open, these species have a jump start on their light-demanding competitors.

This natural drama is continually being played out across the forest landscape. Ecologists and foresters refer to this natural disturbance process as "gap-phase" or "patch dynamics." These

processes are essential to the maintenance of biological diversity, and Carolinian forests are constantly undergoing such dynamic processes and regeneration, most pronounced in stands that are described as "old-growth," where giants and juveniles create an unevenly aged forest.

In addition to allowing higher light levels on the forest floor, gaps also create structural changes to the forest. When produced by blow-downs, gaps end up containing not only felled tree trunks, but also massive tree roots wrenched out of the ground. The resulting "tip-up mounds" create small-scale elevational changes on the forest floor, which produce a hummocky appearance known as pit-and-mound topography. These features are so integral to the health of the forest that they are used by ecologists to help assess the degree to which a forest stand has been left in its natural state. A little more moisture here, and perhaps a little less there, creates the mix of conditions needed to support a variety of plant species. Adding even more structural diversity to these openings are the decaying fallen logs. They provide nurse sites for the seedlings of tree species such as Eastern Hemlock and Yellow Birch, which take advantage of these organically rich and moisture-retaining micro sites in order to get established. Without the benefits of the raised log on which to

The forests of Carolinian Canada are dynamic places of continuous change. Shifting light levels, the result of old trees dying, allow young saplings to soar in their search for sun.

Chinquapin Oak is an adaptable species that grows in diverse habitats, from swamp forests to savannas and alvars.

perch, tiny seedlings can quickly get buried by leaf litter at ground level. Much of the plant diversity in Carolinian forests is synchronized to the pattern and cycles of this natural evolutionary process, and while the scale and frequency of gap formation may vary from wetter to drier sites, all Carolinian forests share this rejuvenating dynamic. Dead and dying trees also diversify the forest ecosystem before they fall. For example, standing dead trees provide food and nesting habitat for many wildlife species — from Pileated Woodpeckers which excavate for carpenter ants to Eastern Screech Owls which nest in tree cavities.

Aside from gaps scattered through the forest, another important structural element of some Carolinian forests is the sub-canopy — the small-tree-and-tall-shrub layer. Most often it is characterized by species adapted to the lower light environment beneath the overstorey. Many plants have adapted to this lower light environment by arranging their leaves on stems in a horizontal branching architecture that maximizes the amount of light that the plants can intercept. One of the most celebrated members of the sub-canopy group is Eastern Flowering Dogwood, a small tree most often found on dry slopes and knolls. Heralding the warmer weather of mid-spring with its tiny flowers surrounded by much larger and showy white, or more rarely pink, petal-like bracts, this Carolinian species occupies a place of honour with naturalists and gardeners alike. It comes into bloom just prior to the leafing-out of the oak canopy above, providing a spectacular spring display.

Growing in the forest understorey or along woodland edges, the forked twigs of Witch-hazel have long been used by diviners to "witch" for water. Witch-hazel's fragrant flowers appear in late autumn and have explosive seeds that can launch themselves up to several metres.

On the forest floor, a myriad of perennial plants have also adapted their life cycles to take advantage of the early spring conditions beneath the leafless canopy. Most prominent where the forest floor consists of moist, loamy, organic-rich soils, plants such as Trout Lily, Red and White Trilliums, Spring Beauty, Mayapple, several species of Violet, Canada Mayflower, and Toothworts can create a veritable carpet of green. Some species die back quickly once the tree canopy above leafs out and diminishes the amount of nurturing sunlight. At the opposite end of the growing season, Witch-hazel, which can attain small-tree status in Carolinian Canada, provides a more subtle autumn flowering display. Its fall yellow bloom provides rich contrast to the ripening scarlet-coloured fruit of the dogwood, which in turn tempts fall-migrating songbirds with a meal in exchange for dispersal of the dogwood's seeds. These understorey trees are most pronounced beneath the canopies of mixed oak and hickory forests found on many sites characterized by well-drained sands or gravelly loams. Common tree

The swamp forests of the sand plain in South Walsingham near Long Point provide habitat for a wide range of creatures, including many species of reptiles and amphibians.

species in these mixed oak-hickory forests include Red, White, and Black Oaks; Bitternut, Pignut, and Shagbark Hickories; along with Red Maple and White Pine.

In swamp forests, or where moisture is in good supply, are other oaks and hickories, including Shumard Oak, Chinquapin Oak, Pin Oak, Swamp White Oak, and Shellbark Hickory. Most of these species rarely dominate the forests in which they are found, and some, like Shellbark Hickory, are quite restricted in their Carolinian range. Beneath these swamp-forest canopies, Spicebush often prevails and can form dense thickets, intermingling with Highbush Blueberry and Buttonbush where more light penetrates the forest canopy. When crushed or bruised, the freshly emerged leaves of Spicebush release a pungent, vaguely lemony smell that adds to the musty aromas of its moist environment. Beneath these small trees and shrubs on the moist forest floor are the tropical-like leaves of Skunk Cabbage, the earliest plant to flower, and one of the few that can actually generate heat. It often begins growing in February amid seeps and springs that have kept the ground from freezing hard.

Bordering streams, the strangely mottled and flaking bark of larger tree trunks signals the presence of American Sycamore. At maturity, sycamore is among the largest living trees in eastern North America. Most prevalent in the riparian forests bordering waterways, these trees have leaves as large as dinner plates, and some in fact can reach the size of serving trays. Sadly, their branches can be seriously disfigured by anthracnose, a fungus that is most troublesome after a cool, wet stretch of weather in the spring, when newly leafed-out trees can be virtually defoliated.

Vivid in autumn, when its leaves turn yellow, orange, red, or purple, Black Gum grows in wet sites and is often associated with other moisture-loving trees such as Swamp White Oak, Silver Maple, and Pumpkin Ash. Its blue-black fruit is eaten by foxes, deer, Raccoons, Virginia Opossums, and many bird species. Some Black Gum trees are more than 450 years old.

Many introduced pathogens from temperate forests elsewhere in the world are threatening the forests of Carolinian Canada. Perhaps the most spectacular example is Chestnut blight, an introduced fungus that, in only a couple of decades early in the last century, reduced the majestic American Chestnut from a state of dominance in many forest stands to now just occasional stump sprouts, some of which still struggle to survive. Perhaps better remembered is the similar decline of another group of common deciduous trees of southern Ontario — the elm. American Elm suffered great losses following the accidental introduction of Dutch elm disease.

For the past decade, new invasive pests in Ontario have continued to threaten the future of trees such as Butternut, Eastern Flowering Dogwood, American Beech, and all of the ash species, including two uncommon Carolinian specialties — Blue and Pumpkin Ash. An outbreak of alien Asian Long-horned Beetle, which attacks a variety of deciduous tree species, is being carefully monitored and may be under control for now, but it, too, could have a devastating impact on Carolinian forests.

Invasive exotic plant species are likewise threatening Carolinian forests. Garlic Mustard, for example, can outcompete and even chemically suppress and disrupt native species. It emerges quickly in spring and covers the whole forest floor, altering conditions for tree-seedling establishment and diminishing light levels for native spring ephemerals. In the case

Above: One of the daintiest spring ephemeral plants of the woodland floor, Dutchman's Breeches, blooms with pendulous "pantaloon" flowers, then goes dormant for the summer. Bumblebees, equipped with the long, specialized mouth parts required to reach this flower's nectaries, are its main nectar feeders and pollinators.

Below: The Dundas Valley is one of the most diverse areas along the Niagara Escarpment and is home to many Carolinian species, including a nationally significant forest bird community. An extensive, forty-kilometre trail system maintained by the Hamilton Conservation Authority winds its way through the valley.

of Oriental Bittersweet, a vigorous woody vine, it simply smothers or strangles the host plant upon which it climbs. Among the worst alien invaders is the Common Buckthorn, which has become a real menace to some Carolinian woodlands. In places, it can take over and dominate the understorey.

While successive invasions by alien species continue to jeopardize the future composition and health of the Carolinian forest, these threats are just one of many challenges for the forests of this ecoregion. Today, air photos and satellite images — not to mention the occasional countryside ramble — illustrate how "successful" modern civilization has been in reducing the Carolinian forest landscape. Now, two hundred years after the clearing of land by European settlers began in earnest, upwards of 80 to 90 percent of the original woodland cover has been lost, and virtually no unaltered old-growth stands remain. In the extreme southwest of the province, both Essex and Kent counties have lost more than 95 percent of their original woodland cover. More easterly counties, such as Norfolk, Haldimand, and Brant, have much higher woodland cover, but much of this is replacement or regenerated forest, that differs in composition and structure from the pre-settlement Carolinian forest.

Large-scale forest clearing has caused serious degradation of water, air, soil, and habitat quality. For plant communities, the "edge

effect" is particularly acute across the region where most forests are small, isolated, and fragmented. Along the edge of a woodlot, environmental conditions are quite different from those in the forest "interior." The subtlety of changes in temperature, humidity, light levels, soil composition, and moisture levels may not be obvious to a casual human visitor, but to forest flora and fauna these changes are significant. Edges also provide easy access points for the entry of invasive species and are often known by botanists to be the "weediest" parts of woodlots. These altered conditions can extend one hundred to two hundred metres into the forest. Given the impact of all of these factors it comes as no surprise that the Carolinian region is home to some of the highest concentrations of species at risk in the country, more than 40 percent of which are plants.

On a brighter note, significant efforts are under way to protect remaining Carolinian forests, guided by a better understanding of the importance and complexity of the region's woodlands. The ecological value of large forest areas, especially with respect to interior habitat and the protection of watersheds, is being recognized, and conservation efforts are better able to focus on areas and actions that have maximum benefit for nature and the environment. Throngs of landowners, youth groups, conservation organizations, and governmental agencies are putting their shoulders to the task of trying to re-establish and reconnect the forests of the Carolinian region. These efforts often advance one hand-planted tree at a time, as people work to protect and restore an ecological legacy in southern Canada.

AS SPRING TURNS TO summer in Carolinian Canada, the southern feel of this paradise becomes most evident. The cathedral canopy of the maple and beech forest fills in, obscuring the view of Tulip-tree flowers and screening out sunlight at the forest floor, and spring wildflowers set fruit and wane. Summer's oppressive heat and humidity are especially noticeable in swamp forests, which buzz with the sounds of cicadas and mosquitoes — or perhaps with a loud refrain from

Top: Bloodroot, named for the orange-red juice found in its stem and rhizome, is one of the first woodland flowers to appear in spring, and often grows with Hepatica, Trout Lily, Dutchman's Breeches, and Spring Beauty. Bloodroot seeds are dispersed by ants.

Above: Found in dry or open woodlands, Wild Columbine attracts hummingbirds to its distinctive, drooping flowers. The long, upturned spurs contain the nectaries, rendering the nectar out of reach to all except long-tongued moths, butterflies, and hummingbirds.

One of the first plants to emerge in late winter and very early spring, Skunk Cabbage generates heat through a chemical reaction within the plant, allowing it to poke up through the snow in forest seepages. Its strong odour, reminiscent of rotting meat, attracts insects.

the rare and elusive Prothonotary Warbler. Wooded ravines, carved by meandering streams, provide contrast to other parts of the forest, particularly where cooler, north-facing slopes are flanked with Eastern Hemlock and other species that hint of Canada's more widespread, northerly forest floras. In late October and early November, the bright yellow Tulip-tree leaves are among the last to make their descent, fluttering to the ground or getting caught in the currents of creeks quickened again with fall rains. Then, even before winter is fully played out, the Carolinian forest stirs to life again, as Skunk Cabbage flowers push through melting snow and attract the first of the season's insects. Soon, the buds of beech trees that now shine in purple contrast to the silver pillars of their elephantine trunks will unfurl, heralding the onset of another growing season.

CHAPTER 2

ONTARIO'S PRAIRIE PENINSULA

Allen Woodliffe

A tremendous variety of plants and animals, including more than one hundred provincially rare species of flora, can be found at the Ojibway Prairie Provincial Nature Reserve in Windsor. In summer, the prairie is full of colourful bloom, including Culver's-root, Coreopsis, Flowering Spurge, and Showy Tick-trefoil.

THE RED FLAMES SWEPT across the prairie landscape, roaring, dancing, and leaping, consuming almost everything in their path. Only a few months before, this place was ablaze — not with fire but with colour — the reds, yellows, oranges, blues, mauves, and whites of prairie wildflowers against a backdrop of majestic swaying grasses and huge open-grown trees. But on this particular day, fire was working its magic during a prescribed

Just a few weeks after a controlled burn at the Ojibway Prairie Provincial Nature Reserve, the landscape regenerates as new green shoots begin to appear in response to the warmed soil and the rejuvenating power of fire.

burn at Ojibway Prairie Provincial Nature Reserve in Windsor, regenerating the prairie landscape.

Ontario is not generally considered a "prairie province," yet it had, and still has, some of the richest and most diverse tallgrass prairie and oak savanna in North America. Early eighteenth- and nineteenth-century travellers described a landscape of extensive "meadows." In 1792, the land surveyor Patrick McNiff described the area along the Thames River between its mouth and the current city of Chatham: "On each side and for a distance upstream of six miles were extensive meadows and marshes without any wood except for a few scattered trees. To the Dover side the meadows and marshes extended north northeast as far as the eye could see."

Tallgrass prairie and oak savanna, jointly referred to as tallgrass communities, are not limited to southwestern Ontario. They also occur in the Rice Lake Plains area of central Ontario and the Rainy River area of the northwest. However, the most extensive and species-rich areas are in the Carolinian zone. Many people are unaware of the occurrence of tallgrass prairie and savanna in Ontario, because the majority of it here — as well as throughout its North American range — was destroyed well over a century ago. When pioneers from the east emerged from the heavily forested Appalachian regions and first encountered these mostly treeless landscapes, they believed that a soil too poor to support trees wouldn't be much good for farming. However, once they realized that the characteristics of these treeless landscapes were a result of fire, and indeed that the soil was very good, the steel moldboard plough had been created to cut through the dense sod. In the fight between plough and prairie, the plough won: today, less than 2 percent of the prairies' original extent remains in Ontario.

PRAIRIE DIVERSITY

Tallgrass communities are a mosaic of tall, robust grasses, hardy wildflowers (or forbs), and a variety of shrubs and trees, all of

Fire plays an essential role in the health of tallgrass prairie and savanna. At the Karner Blue Sanctuary volunteer stewards with Lambton Wildlife Inc. burn the savanna landscape to restore habitat for Wild Blue Lupines, the food plant for the Karner Blue butterfly.

The prairies of Walpole Island are ablaze with colour in the summer, including the magenta spikes of Dense Blazing-star.

which are dependent on what seems a disastrous event: fire. The regular occurrence of fire is essential for the establishment and continued health of tallgrass communities. Fire kills or at least suppresses competing non-prairie plants, especially woody growth. A typical prairie fire travels quickly across the landscape. The black ashes left on the open soil surface after a spring fire absorb the sun's energy, gently warming the soil to a temperature that stimulates the prairie plants to begin their growth. Fire also recycles the nutrients back into the soil much more quickly than does decomposition.

In the past, fire occurred naturally, through lightning strikes, or was started by aboriginal people. An electrical storm could easily strike a lone oak tree, travel to the ground, and ignite the nearby dry grasses. Native people used fire for many purposes: to drive game into hunting grounds; to stimulate the growth of medicinal plants; to reduce fire hazards around their camps; or to defend themselves against enemies. One of the native tribes that lived in the heart of the tallgrass prairie region was the Pottawatomie, which, loosely translated, means "people of the place of fire." Today, their ancestors continue the tradition of burning prairies on Walpole Island, one of the largest and finest examples of tallgrass prairie and oak savanna remaining in Canada.

In addition to fire, drought and animal grazers likely influence the prairie vegetation, though the precise effects are as yet unknown. The principal above-ground grazer of the mid-western prairies — the bison — has never been confirmed as occurring in Ontario. However, underground invertebrate herbivores that are voracious root-feeders, such as the larvae of June Beetles, Click Beetles, and cicadas, are quite abundant.

Prairie specialists have had lively debates trying to agree on precise definitions to distinguish between tallgrass prairie, oak savanna, and oak woodland. Generally, a prairie has fewer than three trees per hectare, while oak savanna is made up of widely spaced, open-grown trees. These ecosystems are very dynamic and will not always fit attempts to define them. What is most important is that these vegetation communities consist of a suite of species, especially grasses and wildflowers, which create conditions for — and actually require the regular occurrence of — fire.

There is a somewhat triangular shape to the configuration of tallgrass prairie and oak savanna in North America, for very good reason. The prevailing winds, especially in the spring, summer, and fall, are from the west and southwest. In the spring, warm winds dry out the previous year's vegetation, and any flames of fire are fanned and directed northeast. Many prairie plants disperse their seeds by wind, so the prevailing winds carry these seeds to new horizons. The expansion of tallgrass prairie moved from the heart of the midwestern part of the continent to the northeast. Southern Ontario is at the apex of this triangular-shaped vegetation community that is sometimes referred to as the "prairie peninsula."

Prior to extensive settlement of the region, there was a constant battle for space between the wide-open prairie and the mature, "climax" beech-maple forest. A beech-maple forest is not fire dependent, nor is it even tolerant of fire. When the flames reached the beech-maple forests, the fine fuels such as grasses were too sparse to let the fire advance any farther, and so the intensity and extent of the fire died out. However, before the fire died out entirely, the edges of the beech-maple forest might have been affected by the flames, creating conditions for more fire-tolerant oaks. The establishment of oaks created conditions for prairie grasses and wildflowers to take hold. If there were long enough periods of regular fire, the oak woodlands might eventually become oak savanna, which in turn might eventually become prairie. (In fact, during the hypsithermal period of about five thousand to eight thousand years ago, the temperatures in southern Ontario were warmer than they are currently. Prairie and savanna undoubtedly flourished, and were possibly more prevalent than they were at the time of European settlement.) Conversely, during extended periods that were less favourable for fire, the beech-maple forest would gain a foothold in the oak woodland and eventually advance into the savanna and prairie.

Adaptation to fire is not the only competitive advantage that prairie plants have. The root systems of many prairie plants also play an important role. Their biomass below ground is much greater than above. Roots typically reach depths of one to two metres below the surface, and some species are known to have roots extending to depths of more than six metres. These depths, which are adaptations to drought, give prairie plants a distinct advantage in obtaining moisture over non-prairie species, whose roots more typically reach only half a metre in depth. As well, these underground energy reserves ensure that prairie plants can survive fire and grazing.

PRAIRIE GRASSES

Approximately thirty-five native grass species can be found on the prairies and savannas of southwestern Ontario, with five species making up the majority: Big Bluestem, Little Bluestem, Switch Grass, Prairie Cord Grass, and Indian Grass. The first three species are "bunch grasses" — the plant starts with only one or two stems, but continues to grow outwardly in a bunch over many decades. Because they produce dense sod and deep root systems, bunch grasses are able to outcompete many other species for both moisture and space and thus are the most dominant. Over time, the extensive root systems provide the organic material required for extremely rich soil production. Some of the best topsoils in the world, sometimes more than 0.6 metres in depth, have developed in prairies.

These five grasses are the essence of prairie, but a number of other species can be found as very minor components. These include Kalm's Brome Grass, found at prairie edges, and Bottlebrush Grass, which prefers savanna. Much rarer are species with enticing names such as Arrow Feather Three Awn, Side-oats Grama, Purple Love Grass, and Prairie Dropseed.

PRAIRIE WILDFLOWERS THROUGH THE SEASONS

As dominant and impressive as the grasses are, the more showy plants are the wildflowers. There is great variety both in form and colour, with a dazzling display of diversity from the earliest flowering wildflowers in late April to the last gasp of colour in November.

Top: Big Bluestem, a signature grass of the tallgrass prairie, has an extensive root system that goes down deep into the soil, allowing it to reach the water table even at very dry sites. Its aboveground growth is also extensive, reaching three metres or more in height.

Left: Little Bluestem, one of the shorter prairie grasses, produces feathery flowers in late summer and autumn. Many larval butterflies, including Dusted Skipper and Indian Skipper, feed on the leaves of this grass.

After a spring fire, there is an almost immediate greening up as the prairie plants rush to take advantage of moisture, nutrients, and space. Some of the first plants to flower are Blue-eyed Grass, Wild Strawberry, and Yellow Star-grass, their foliage and blossoms appearing even while the ground is still covered with ash. Along with the common early bloomers, there are a number of rare species that occur only at a few Ontario sites: Fringed Puccoon is restricted to sandy, red-cedar savannas of Point Pelee and Pelee Island, while the endangered Bird's-foot Violet is found only in the Norfolk Sand Plain region. The largest Ontario population of the endangered Small White Lady's-slipper can be found at Walpole Island, where it can number in the thousands.

These earliest species are usually short, as they grow quickly but only enough to ensure an adequate amount of sunlight energy to achieve flowering. By the time they begin to set seed, taller species are starting to flower. In general, the later in the season the plants flower, the taller they must grow to compete for sunlight.

After this initial spring burst of growth and colour, summer-flowering species dominate the prairie palette. In early June, Hairy Beard-tongue, Smooth Beard-tongue, and Canada Anemone begin flowering. Wood Lily, Wood Vetch, the endangered Purple Twayblade, and Virginia Goat's-rue are inhabitants of some savannas. Butterflyweed's orange glow vividly contrasts with the predominant green of the prairie in early summer and is a hint of the rising crescendo of colour that is to follow in the weeks ahead. The endangered Eastern Prairie Fringed Orchid appears in the less disturbed prairies as June rolls into July, its cluster of delicate white flowers sitting atop a sturdy stem, beckoning to hawkmoths to come and pollinate them. Wild Bergamot, Black-eyed Susan, and Showy Tick-trefoil provide drifts of colour by mid-summer — and plenty of nectar for butterflies. Punctuating the colourful show in drier parts of the prairie are the single white spikes of Colicroot. In moister areas, is the taller, white candelabra-like Culver's-root. Meandering through the luxuriant growth at this time of year can please one's sense of smell, with Mountain-mint exuding a minty fragrance.

From top to bottom: Occasionally, three closely related Lady's-slipper orchids (Small White, Large Yellow, and Small Yellow) will hybridize, creating unusual colour combinations. Butterflyweed provides nectar for many butterfly species, including the Northern Crescent. The deep magenta-red flowers of Purple Milkweed distinguish it from the much paler Common Milkweed. Milkweeds are the larval food plant for the Monarch butterfly. Miami Mist is a very rare species in Canada, restricted to alvars in the Carolinian region.

The last week of July and the first two weeks of August are typically the peak of flowering diversity in most prairies. Many of the earlier July species will continue to flower, but this is the time when the "flagship" prairie and savanna species are most obvious. Gray-headed Coneflower, Prairie Dock, with its huge, sandpapery, spade-like leaves, and Dense Blazing-star with its purple spikes, are three of the most distinctive prairie species.

From mid-August to the end of the flowering season, a parade of sunflowers, goldenrods, and asters gives the prairies a predominantly yellow hue. One of the tallest plants on the prairie is Tall Sunflower which occasionally reaches up to three and a half metres in height. Vying for sunlight along the savanna edges are Woodland, Thin-leaved, and Pale-leaved Sunflowers. Goldenrods, primarily Canada Goldenrod and Tall Goldenrod, dominate the fall prairie landscape, which may also include much rarer goldenrods such as Rigid, Riddell's, and Showy. Asters compete with goldenrods for dominance and include Heath, Sky Blue, Hairy, New England, and Flat-topped Asters. And if one looks past these dominating species, one can find some real gems of colour sprinkled throughout the later flowering period. Widely scattered is Bottle Gentian, with its bright blue "bottle" flowers that bees climb into and then have trouble escaping; rarer is the delicate Fringed Gentian. Even more restricted is the tiny Stiff Gentian, and by far the rarest of all is the Cream Gentian, known only from two remote savannas on Walpole Island.

WOODY PLANTS

The woody species in both prairie and savanna communities are much the same, but the relative importance within the communities varies. Black Oak is the oak most likely to occur, especially on drier sites, along with White Oak, and occasionally Chinquapin, Pin, and Bur Oaks. Mature oaks often have thick bark that is fire resistant and enables these species to survive in a fire-dependent ecosystem. Less fire-resistant, and therefore less common than the oaks, are Shagbark and Pignut Hickories, White Ash, Aspen, American Elm, and the occasional American Sycamore.

Shrubs are the almost forgotten components of the tallgrass communities' vegetation. Many are neither specific to prairie or savanna, nor especially showy. Typical and most abundant

From top to bottom: The rare Cream Gentian is found in Carolinian Canada only on Walpole Island. This Flat-topped White Aster was found amongst Goldenrod and Purple Aster at the Dundas Valley Trail Centre. A plant of wet prairies and meadows, Fringed Gentian blooms in autumn. Prairie Rose is a climbing shrub that grows in prairies, alvars, thickets, clearings, and woodland edges near Lake St. Clair and the western end of Lake Erie.

species include Staghorn Sumac, Fragrant Sumac, Smooth Sumac, Gray Dogwood, Red-osier Dogwood, American Hazel, New Jersey Tea, and even Poison Ivy.

ALVAR COMMUNITIES

There are many similarities between the vegetation found in alvars and prairies, but alvars are a distinct habitat type. An alvar is an area where soil is very shallow (typically about ten centimetres or less), or even non-existent, over limestone or dolostone. This results in a very challenging environment for

Towering oaks and ground-covering ferns flourish at the sandpit savannas of Walpole Island First Nation. The people here steward the largest intact mesic prairie and savanna remnants in the Carolinian region, with several thousand hectares and 12 percent of Canada's species at risk.

One of the best remaining alvars in the Carolinian region, Stone Road Alvar on Pelee Island, is protected by conservation organizations such as Ontario Nature, Essex Region Conservation Authority, and the Nature Conservancy of Canada. A publicly accessible trail leads through a portion of this unique, fascinating habitat.

plants, which can appear almost to be growing on pavement. The soil can be extremely saturated in the spring but bone-dry for extended periods in the heat of mid-summer. The well-developed root systems of many prairie plants enable them to survive in the extremely dry conditions that regularly occur on an alvar, and they find enough moisture in the smallest cracks and crevices. Significant alvar species include Wild Hyacinth, Miami Mist, Nodding Onion, and Alumroot.

Alvars are an extremely rare habitat type: the majority (approximately 75 percent) of the world's alvars are in the Ontario portion of the Great Lakes Basin. Within the Carolinian zone there are some relatively small, but significant, alvar sites, probably totalling fewer than six hundred hectares. Farming, grazing, and quarrying have all had an impact on these alvars.

Portions of Pelee Island, amounting to several hundred hectares, are wonderful examples and unique in the overall scheme of alvars. The best-known site is the Stone Road Alvar, in excess of two hundred hectares, near the southeast corner of the island. Compared with more northern and eastern alvars, primarily on Manitoulin Island, the Bruce Peninsula, and Carden Plain, the amount of exposed limestone on the Pelee Island sites is low, less than 5 percent. However, the soil is quite shallow and prone to extremely wet or extremely dry growing conditions. Woodland and savanna vegetation occurs, although it is sometimes stunted for its age because of the harsh growing conditions. During a study in 1988, for example, a Chinquapin Oak measuring thirty-four centimetres in diameter was determined to be 110 years old.

Despite the harsh conditions of exposed bedrock and thin soils which alternate between extremely wet and dry, plants such as Nodding Wild Onion are able to flourish in the alvars of Carolinian Canada.

THE ORIGINAL TALLGRASS PRAIRIE and savanna quickly fell victim to the plough. It isn't known exactly how extensive these original communities were, but estimates are as high as 140 million hectares across North America; today, less than 5 percent remains, and much less than 1 percent of this is formally protected. In Ontario, prior to European settlement, there were an estimated eighty to two hundred thousand hectares; only 1 to 2 percent remains.

In spite of the bleak past, the future of these endangered communities looks somewhat more hopeful. Conservation agencies and organizations are recognizing the significance of prairies and, in the past three decades, have acquired and protected some of the best remnants. The science and management of these communities is growing, and includes research, conferences, an expanded prescribed-burn program, and the preparation of a formal Recovery Strategy. Groups such as Tallgrass Ontario are advocating for stewardship and protection. Even so, many of the remaining sites are under constant threat due to isolation from other remnants, as well as from invasive species, development pressures, and the lack of adequate funds for management. Yet facsimiles of prairies, in the form of prairie gardens, are reappearing on the landscape, ranging from backyard and school plots to roadsides and even small fields. While planting a small diversity of prairie seeds into former agricultural land does not recreate true prairie, it is an important step towards protecting the genetic diversity of our natural heritage and inspiring and educating our communities about the value of this important habitat.

The future of tallgrass prairie in Ontario depends on the protection of existing remnants and the restoration of degraded sites through prescribed burns and other management techniques. As awareness of Ontario's tallgrass heritage grows, so too does the commitment to conserving this unique landscape.

CHAPTER 3

Wetlands *and* Their Plants

Deborah Metsger

"Rank weeds and lush, slimy water plants sent an odour of decay and a heavy miasmatic vapour into our faces, while a false step plunged us into the dark quivering mire, which shook for yards in soft undulations around our feet."

SIR ARTHUR CONAN DOYLE'S DARK description of a wetland is perhaps one of the most evocative ever written. It encapsulates wetland processes, soil, vegetation, and human ambivalence in a few powerful words. But does it really capture the complex and fascinating nature of wetlands?

The 2,400-hectare Beverly Swamp is one of the largest forested wetlands remaining in southern Ontario. Its survival can be linked, at least in part, to the fear it engendered in early European settlers, who regarded it as a dangerous place — stories of horses disappearing into the muck are part of local lore.

Carolinian Canada is essentially a peninsula surrounded on three sides by major bodies of water: to the west, Lake Huron, the St. Clair River, Lake St. Clair, and the Detroit River; to the south, Lake Erie; and to the east, the Niagara River and Lake Ontario. These are all part of the larger Great Lakes complex.

So much water means that picturesque wetlands and shorelines fringe the margins of Carolinian Canada. These wetlands are iconic for the region, important for the economy and crucial to the rich resident and migratory fauna. The coastal wetlands of Point Pelee, Rondeau Bay, Long Point, Lake St. Clair, and Turkey Point attract throngs of people and millions of passing birds, in addition to the multitudes that live there year round. Prior to European settlement, even more wetlands dotted the landscape, both inland and bordering the many rivers, streams, and lakes. Regrettably, agricultural and urban development have substantially reduced their number and area, but those that remain continue to be a prominent feature of the Carolinian life zone. They play a critical role in maintaining a healthy ecosystem and make an important contribution to the economy and biodiversity of the region.

WHAT ARE WETLANDS AND WHAT DO THEY DO?

Wetlands combine features of both aquatic (water) and terrestrial (dry land) habitats and therefore are frequently described as ecotones, or transition zones, between terrestrial and deep-water aquatic habitats. They have a high biodiversity because they can support both terrestrial and aquatic species, as well as those species that are wetland "specialists."

The essence of wetland plants is that they can withstand

Top: This is a typical Great Lakes coastal shoreline bordering Carolinian Canada.

Left: The boardwalks of Point Pelee National Park offer excellent opportunities to view a vast coastal marsh up close.

"having their feet wet" for long periods. This creates several challenges for plants, the most important of which is the low supply of oxygen received by roots in saturated soils. Many wetland plants have special structures and mechanisms that bring oxygen to their roots, but life for plants in ecotones also involves surviving and adapting to constant change and consequent stress. Under natural conditions, the water level in wetlands fluctuates widely. This takes place both annually, with high water levels in spring and "draw down" in late summer, and on multi-year cycles, which are controlled by broader climate patterns. Although boaters and cottagers may consider such fluctuations to be a curse, wetland plants are not only adapted to these conditions, but require them for establishment and renewal.

When wetland plants reproduce, their seeds are dispersed by water, wind, or wildlife, then sink to the bottom and are stored in the soil, perhaps for years. During periods of low water, the seeds are exposed and start to germinate, spreading new, green life above the waterline. If low water persists, shrubs and other dry-land plants inexorably invade the shore, but the next high water drowns the invaders and allows the wetland species to reign once more. Only wetland shrubs like Buttonbush and Silky Dogwood will survive the inundation, and so the cycle begins again.

The role of wetlands in the landscape cannot be overstated.

Some of the most extensive Great Lakes coastal wetlands are protected at Rondeau Provincial Park, along Lake Erie.

Dense mats of submerged aquatic plants teem with wildlife including this passing Eastern Gartersnake.

They carry out a number of very important ecological functions that help moderate extremes in the terrestrial environment. First and foremost is their role in the water cycle. In early spring there are heavy rains and runoff from melting snow. Wetlands, especially flood plains adjacent to rivers and streams, help to regulate water flow, serving as a sponge by sopping up flood water, a process referred to as groundwater recharge. The stored water is gradually released over the summer and helps prevent streams from drying out. Secondly, wetlands act as water-purification systems that filter contaminants. The mechanisms that wetland plants use for accumulating oxygen enhance their ability to trap minerals and nutrients, and also create a suitable environment for micro-organisms that assist with the breakdown of organic matter and even harmful bacteria and viruses. Thirdly, wetlands are very productive ecosystems: that is, they are very efficient at converting the sun's energy into biomass. Hence, above and below the water, they provide rich habitat for an abundance of wildlife species – fishes, molluscs and other invertebrates, insects, birds, reptiles, amphibians, and mammals.

Thick walls of impenetrable cattails line small channels through the coastal wetlands of Carolinian Canada.

Wetlands also provide income, livelihoods, recreation, beauty, research opportunities, and education for people.

What is astonishing is that, given all the benefits that they provide, wetlands have historically been despised by people. For millennia humans have regarded and treated wetlands as wastelands, too wet to use for growing crops or building on, difficult to navigate, and full of "pests." Ever since the technology has been available, wetlands have been drained to create dry land or dredged to create ponds or shipping channels. The prevailing attitude was that this was the only way to make them useful. Wetland conversion was common practice until the later decades of the twentieth century, when people, and governments, began to realize that wetlands are crucial to maintain water supplies and to sustain biodiversity.

WETLAND COMMUNITY TYPES

Wetlands are categorized according to the substrate (mineral or organic soil, or peat) and by the kinds of plants that grow in them. Major wetland types include: swamps; marshes; wet

Top: The stout trunks of maple trees are reflected in the vernal pools of Potawatami swamp, Walpole Island First Nation.

Above: In midsummer, the spherical flower clusters of Buttonbush grace thicket swamps such as those found in Backus Woods.

meadows; and peatlands such as bogs and fens.

For the most part, wetlands in Carolinian Canada and their associated wetland plants are not restricted to the zone, but rather are similar to those found throughout the Great Lakes region. The exceptions include specific wetland communities such as wet oak systems and thicket swamps, some of which are globally rare. What is distinctive about Carolinian wetlands is that they exhibit greater biodiversity than do those in ecoregions farther north. Plant species with distributions that reach far to the north mingle with southern species that are at the extreme northern limit of their range to increase the diversity of Carolinian wetlands. In addition, plants such as Poison Ivy grow in wetlands in Carolinian Canada, but farther north are wholly terrestrial. The longer growing season in the south gives such plants time to flower and set seed under cooler wetland conditions.

Swamps

Wetlands on mineral soil or well-decomposed organic matter, and which are dominated by trees or shrubs, are called swamps and thicket swamps, respectively. Swamps typically form on nutrient-rich lowlands or flood plains, often as part of a larger forested system. They frequently have vernal pools that form in

the spring but are bone dry by late summer and fall. Swamps are found throughout Carolinian Canada where they occupy lowlands in forested areas and form complex mosaics with upland forests. In many cases, swamps have survived land clearing because of the extra effort needed to drain them and convert them to agriculture.

Floating mats of Yellow Water-lily leaves stand out amongst the sedges and submerged aquatic plants that line the edges of marshes and ponds.

OPEN WETLANDS

Some of the most abundant wetlands of Carolinian Canada border the region's lakes, rivers, and streams. They are open and treeless, dominated by herbaceous (non-woody) plants, and range from watery marshes to seasonally inundated wet meadows. Emergent plants — so called because they are rooted in the water, but their leaves and stems extend above the water surface — dominate marshes.

The most extensive wetlands remaining in Carolinian Canada are the Great Lakes Coastal Wetlands that lie along the shorelines of the Great Lakes and their waterways. They are directly

influenced by natural and regulated water-level fluctuations in the Great Lakes Basin. The sheltered coasts of the Lake Erie sand spits — Point Pelee, Long Point, Turkey Point, and Rondeau — and the delta of the St. Clair River exemplify the coastal wetlands found within Carolinian Canada. These large wetlands buffer the mainland from the potentially harsh impacts of water and wind and provide critical habitat for a wealth of wildlife.

Marshes, composed mainly of large stands of a single species, stretch for kilometres, forming irregular lake margins. Patches of tall cattails and Giant Reed Grass create impenetrable walls of vegetation. The clear turquoise waters of the deepest channels interweave with channels and bays that are filled with submerged aquatic plants, including pondweeds, milfoils, Water Buttercup, Coontail, Water Star-grass, and Tape-grass. Most of these plants have tiny flowers that sit atop a tangled mass of underwater vegetation, which provides critical food and shelter for fishes, turtles, and invertebrates, but wreaks havoc with the propellers of passing boats.

Mats of yellow Pond-lily and White Water-lily have large, flat, floating leaves and are interspersed with the smaller oval leaves and pink flowers of Water Smartweed and Watershield. Occasionally one is lucky enough to observe the rare American Lotus, with its magnificent flowers and large, nearly round leaves that either float on the water surface or are held erect. This plant is probably best recognized for its conical, flat-topped seed heads, which are sold commercially for dried-flower arrangements. Like other species of Lotus that are sacred in Hindu and Buddhist cultures, the American Lotus is considered sacred by several Native American cultures and is said to have mystic powers.

Stands of sedges, sombre bulrushes, white-flowered arrowheads, and brilliant blue-purple Pickerel-weed provide splashes of colour to marshes in their flowering seasons. Wild Rice leaves float languidly on the water surface, but in summer the flowering spikes emerge from the surface and stand upright. In fall the seeds serve as food for huge flocks of waterfowl and other migrating birds, and provide important economic support for a number of First Nations people.

From top to bottom: American Grass-of-Parnassus is a delicate plant found in calcareous habitats including wet meadows, marshes, and fens. A bumblebee visits a bright yellow Sneezeweed flower. American Lotus is one of Carolinian Canada's most spectacular aquatic plants, with distinctive round leaves that rise above the water, fragrant pale yellow flowers, and woody seed pods that are often used in flower arrangements. The striking blue-purple flowers of Pickerel-weed can be seen in shallow waters from June to September.

On higher ground, the large, pink, bowl-shaped blossoms of Swamp Rose Mallow stand tall against the blue sky and the greens, browns, and yellows of the marsh. This large woody perennial is one of the most northerly representatives of a sizeable tropical family, and the only member of the genus *Hibiscus* that occurs naturally in the wild in Canada, where it is a threatened species. Most flowers last a single day and are usually pollinated by bumblebees.

Where the water meets the land wet meadows are formed, and change their nature across the years and throughout the season in response to water levels. Some wet meadows are dominated mainly by sedges and rushes, but others contain rich mixtures of grasses, including the native variety of the Giant Reed Grass, which First Nations people call "Red Legs," and colourful forbs like bright yellow Sneezeweed, deep blue gentians, and white Grass-of-Parnassus.

Top: Swamp Rose Mallow grows amongst the cattails in the marshes of the St. Clair River Delta.

Above: The large pink flowers and robust buds of the Swamp Rose Mallow stand out against its dark green heart-shaped leaves.

PEATLANDS

Peatlands are wetlands with an accumulation of undecomposed organic matter. Peatlands are rare in Carolinian Canada, because the warmer temperatures, flat terrain, and well-drained soils that are characteristic of the region are not conducive to the buildup of organic matter that leads to the development of peatlands in

This floating bog mat in Sifton Bog, a 30-hectare wetland complex within the City of London, supports ericaceous shrubs and coniferous trees that are rare to Carolinian Canada but typical of more northerly wetlands.

the north. Thus, in Carolinian Canada, peatlands are found only on isolated sites that hold water. Bogs are acidic peatlands where Sphagnum moss provides the substrate, controls the water chemistry, and isolates the wetland from the influences of groundwater. Treed bogs support coniferous species like Black and White Spruce and Tamarack, which are common in the north, but found in the Carolinian life zone only in rare and scattered peatlands.

Two notable examples of peatlands in Carolinian Canada are Sifton Bog and Wainfleet Bog. Sifton Bog, in the City of London, developed in a kettle hole — a deep depression formed when a chunk of ice was left behind in the deposits of a retreating glacier. Wainfleet Bog in Niagara sits perched in a shallow depression on the Haldimand Clay Plain. When the ice sheet retreated from the region, the Onondaga escarpment blocked drainage to Lake Erie, and a wetland complex formed.

The cool, nutrient-poor conditions in the Sifton and Wainfleet wetlands mimic the conditions of peatlands in the boreal forests of the north. These are among the few places in Carolinian Canada where one can experience the wonders of a northern peatland. Plumes of Cotton-grass sway in the wind; sundews and Pitcher Plants trap insects to augment their diet in these nutrient-poor habitats; and northern, acid-loving shrubs of the heath family, such as Leatherleaf, Bog-rosemary, and Labrador-tea, abound. Highbush Blueberry is another member of the heath family, but its range extends not north, but southwards. It grows in peatlands and swamps across Carolinian Canada, sometimes forming pure thickets in peaty sloughs and kettle depressions. Many varieties of cultivated blueberries are derived from this species. Peatlands in the Great Lakes area also host a small tree that may well be the most dangerous plant found in Carolinian Canada. Poison Sumac is related to Poison Ivy, and like that species produces a clear sap that can cause a severe dermatitis of itchy rashes and blisters.

THREATS AND PROMISES FOR CAROLINIAN WETLANDS

When Elizabeth Simcoe, wife of Upper Canada's first governor, arrived in 1792 in what is now Toronto, the harbour was bordered by wetlands that extended from the base of the Scarborough Bluffs all the way to the mouth of the Humber River. Virtually all of these Toronto wetlands have now been lost to development. Since European settlement, the majority of the natural wetlands throughout Carolinian Canada have been drained and cleared for agriculture and urban development. Wetlands once covered more than 25 percent of the region; today they occupy less than 5 percent.

The past thirty years have seen an awakening to the importance of wetlands to the wellbeing of people and to the economy. Significant efforts have been directed toward protecting

Wild Rice marshes are of cultural and economic importance to First Nations. This marsh is at Rondeau Provincial Park.

Many Carolinian wetlands were drained to make way for agriculture and development. Those that remain constitute a small percentage of the rural environment.

the wetlands that remain in Carolinian Canada, but development pressures continue. In spite of recognition and protection of some wetlands in planning documents like the Provincial Policy Statement, there is still pressure to develop marinas and housing along lakeshores and to use natural wetlands as storm-water-management facilities. In addition, the health of wetlands is threatened by the regulation of water levels in the Great Lakes for shipping and flood control. Dikes that are built to create habitat for migrating waterfowl moderate natural water fluctuations and reduce the flow of nutrients and organisms in and out of wetlands. Global warming models predict a reduction in precipitation that will lead to lower water levels for prolonged periods. Melting ice sheets originally filled the Great Lakes, and much of the volume is made up of non-replaceable fossil water. Finally, there is an ongoing threat from invasive species. Luckily, Purple Loosestrife, once considered an insurmountable threat in disturbed inland wetlands, seems to be on the decline, perhaps due to the introduction of beetles that are its natural predators in Europe. Now, non-native varieties of Giant Reed Grass are encroaching on wetlands in

Carolinian Canada and throughout North America. They appear to respond vigorously to increased nitrogen deposition from the atmosphere as a consequence of air pollution and from surface water pollution. Giant Reed Grass is so tall and robust that it quickly dwarfs and outcompetes the native grasses, sedges, and other wetland plants that provide shelter and food for wildlife. Likewise, vigorous Hybrid Cattail forms pure stands and is having a similar impact. Who knows what the next invader may be.

Despite these threats and ongoing challenges, there is much to celebrate about wetlands in Carolinian Canada. Conservation Authorities in the region have responded to development pressures with strong wetland policies designed to protect and enhance the wetlands that remain and to focus attention on the

This image of a channel through the St. Clair River Delta of the Walpole Island First Nation shows the progression from native emergent plants at the water's edge to the wall of non-native Giant Reed Grass in the background.

Along the Great Lakes shorelines, marshes and ponds are often nestled behind the dunes.

health of watersheds as a whole. The Wetland Drain Restoration Project is an example of a successful partnership between private landowners, provincial agencies, and regional governments that has promoted sustainable water use and led to the restoration of numerous wetlands in Norfolk County and elsewhere. Finally, through the combined efforts of conservation organizations, government agencies, and First Nations, a significant proportion of the wetlands that remain have been set aside and protected as parks or wildlife reserves. Some wetlands in Carolinian Canada are recognized globally. Long Point is a Biosphere Reserve. Point Pelee and the St. Clair Marshes are included among Canada's thirty-seven wetlands that have been listed as globally important by the RAMSAR Convention (an intergovernmental treaty designed to foster planning and protection for wetlands worldwide). Carolinian Canada may be a small corner of the world, but it harbours global treasures.

PART II

THE ANIMALS OF CAROLINIAN CANADA

Introduction *to* Part II

Michelle Kanter

Previous page: Scarlet Tanager can be found in forests throughout Carolinian Canada. The female's plumage is less colourful than the male's.

Below: Though commonly seen in Carolinian Canada, the Monarch butterfly has been designated a species of special concern due to habitat destruction of its wintering grounds in Mexico. The migratory feat of this species' long journey to Mexico was, until relatively recently, a mystery with many unanswered questions.

CAROLINIAN CANADA HAS a wild diversity of animal life and is home to species found nowhere else in Canada. The animals of the Carolinian region fill a multitude of niches and habitats. Each of the plant communities described in Part I supports distinctive animal life. In our "deep woods," you may find rare birds and flying squirrels particularly adapted to old-growth trees. In prairies and savannas and old fields, the elusive Northern Bobwhite is fighting for survival. Roadside meadows are alive with hundreds of butterfly species in the summer. As many fishers know, beneath the water's surface lies a treasure trove of interesting and important fishes, shellfish, turtles, and many other aquatic inhabitants. Even beach dunes are important habitat for sand-loving species, such as the Fowler's Toad.

From the earliest times, when First Nations used fire to clear vegetation for hunting, humans have created clearings. Today, open spaces dominate the landscape. This habitat has attracted many species that require open spaces, typically wildlife from western grasslands, such as Coyotes, that proliferate in Carolinian Canada's cultural landscape.

At one time, Carolinian Canada was home to Lynx, Bobcat, and the Karner Blue butterfly that no longer inhabit the region. As you will read in the pages that follow, many other interesting, beautiful, and ecologically important species of the Carolinian zone are at risk in Ontario, dependent on shrinking habitat.

Carolinian Canada supports a unique and diverse kaleidoscope of animal life that many people would be surprised to find at their doorstep. With thousands of faunal species, this region has more wildlife than most of the rest of Canada. These pages introduce you to a few of our wild neighbours.

CHAPTER 4

MAMMALS: FROM BATS *to* BADGERS

Sandy Dobbyn

PEOPLE SEE WILD MAMMALS almost every day of their lives, but just a few species, such as Eastern Gray Squirrels, Eastern Chipmunks, and Raccoons, constitute the vast majority of those mammal encounters in the Carolinian region. Most other mammals tend to be more secretive and hide from us by being nocturnal, remaining under cover, or simply shying away from human activity. As a result, many of us would be surprised to know that, in the Carolinian zone, you can find fifty of Ontario's seventy-nine extant mammal species.

Of these fifty species, forty-six are native to Ontario, while three are European introductions (Norway Rat, House Mouse, and European Hare) and one (Eastern Fox Squirrel) was

Unlike squirrels, the Eastern Chipmunk hibernates, spending winters in underground burrows that it excavates in such a way that no traces are left to let their predators know their whereabouts. It is a sure sign of spring when chipmunks appear.

introduced from Ohio. The Norway Rat and House Mouse tend to be restricted to urban and agricultural areas, and are therefore rarely found in natural habitats. Conversely, the European Hare is now a common mammal of fields and open woodlots throughout southern Ontario, and Eastern Fox Squirrels are well established on Pelee Island.

A number of other mammals were found in the Carolinian zone prior to European settlement, but eventually disappeared as a result of habitat loss and fragmentation, over-hunting, and persecution. For example, the eastern subspecies of Wapiti or Elk ranged throughout much of eastern North America, including southern Ontario, as far north as Lake Nipissing. Excessive hunting and habitat loss resulted in the complete loss of the eastern subspecies from Canada by 1850, and eventually led to its extinction. More recently, the western race of Wapiti was introduced to Ontario, though not to the Carolinian zone.

Many of the other mammal species that have been lost from the Carolinian zone were predators that suffered significantly from persecution: for example, the Lynx, Bobcat, Mountain Lion, and Black Bear. The Lynx, Bobcat, and Black Bear retreated to the north, while the Mountain Lion has been extirpated from the majority of the province including the Carolinian zone. Occasionally a Black Bear, Lynx, or Bobcat may wander south

into the Carolinian zone, but these individuals are considered vagrants rather than residents. The River Otter was also once found in the northern reaches of the Carolinian zone, particularly in the northeast corner, but the degradation of streams and lakes eventually resulted in otters all but disappearing from the zone.

There are very few mammal species that are restricted entirely to the Carolinian zone. Even the Virginia Opossum, which many people consider to be the quintessential Carolinian species, ranges well north of the zone, as far as Grey and Bruce counties and the Muskokas. The mammals that are currently restricted to the Carolinian

The Red Fox can be seen in fields hunting in an "ambush style," like a cat. It pounces on small rodents such as meadow voles and mice, coming down on prey with all four feet.

zone in Ontario are the Eastern Mole, Woodland Vole, and Least Shrew.

The following profiles include a selection of mammals found in the Carolinian region.

The diet of the Virginia Opossum, Canada's only marsupial, is varied and includes small mammals, birds, eggs, insects, and fruit.

VIRGINIA OPOSSUM

The Virginia Opossum is North America's only marsupial (meaning that the female has an external abdominal pouch where the young develop, similar to a kangaroo). Young are born in an incomplete stage of development, after a gestation of only twelve or thirteen days, and then make their way to the pouch, where they attach to a nipple and continue development for about ten weeks.

Opossums are the size of a large house cat, with a long, narrow snout and a prehensile tail. The opossum is the only mammal in Ontario (other than humans) with an opposable thumb, but in the case of the opossum, it is on the hind foot. This allows them to grasp and manipulate objects with a high degree of dexterity. For example, the thumb and prehensile tail are both used for grasping branches while climbing. When threatened by potential predators, such as dogs, Coyotes, humans, or foxes, opossums will often feign death, rolling onto their backs with their tongues hanging out — hence the phrase "playing possum."

Opossums are nocturnal, and their habitat is diverse, ranging from forests to urban areas. They do not hibernate, though during bouts of cold weather they do take shelter in hollow trees,

Ontario's Coyotes are a mix of Timber Wolf and western Coyote, and often have pack-like tendencies, unlike the Coyotes found in the U.S. Midwest.

logs, other animal burrows, and even buildings. The range of the opossum fluctuates with winter intensity. A prolonged period of mild winters will result in an increase of their range to the north, while one or two long, cold winters can almost eliminate opossums from the northern extent of their range, and even the province as a whole. In fact, opossums colonized Ontario at least four times between 1850 and 1947. Since that time, climate warming and milder winters have allowed opossums to persist and expand their range farther than they ever have in the past.

LEAST SHREW

At a mere five grams (about the weight of a quarter), the Least Shrew rivals the Pygmy Shrew as North America's smallest mammal (the Pygmy Shrew is about the weight of a dime). The Least Shrew is known in Ontario from only a handful of records at Long Point on the north shore of Lake Erie and from a single record in the Dundas–Ancaster area. South of Lake Erie, in the United States, it inhabits grassy, weedy, or brushy vegetation, and is not found in forests. At Long Point, it was found inhabiting vegetated dunes and grassy areas near marshes. Although this species has not been found elsewhere in Ontario, it is particularly difficult to trap and may simply have gone unnoticed. There are a number of areas along the Lake Erie coast with suitable habitat where this elusive mammal could be found.

EASTERN MOLE

Although common throughout the eastern United States, in Canada the Eastern Mole is restricted to Essex County and the west end of Kent County. It has a long nose with upturned nostrils, massive front feet with strong claws, and an almost hairless tail. Both the front and hind feet are webbed.

The largest of Ontario's three mole species, the Eastern Mole is almost completely subterranean, and thus rarely seen. They dig extensive tunnel systems in soft, moist, sandy and sandy-loam soils, where they feed on soil invertebrates such as earthworms and insect larvae. They can dig up to five metres of tunnel per hour, and their tunnellings and "push ups" are conspicuous features of their woodland habitat, particularly in the spring, before the emergence of herbaceous vegetation. Soil modification by agriculture has, however, rendered some areas of Essex County unsuitable for Eastern Moles. This, combined with their overall restricted range in Ontario, has led to this species being designated as of special concern.

EASTERN PIPISTRELLE

The Eastern Pipistrelle is slightly smaller than the Little Brown Bat, with tricoloured fur on its back and black wing membranes with a contrasting flesh- or orange-coloured forearm. Pipistrelles are common south of the Great Lakes in the eastern United States, but are relatively uncommon in Carolinian Canada. Eastern Pipistrelles hibernate in caves and mines, and tend not to disperse as far from hibernation sites as other bats. This may limit their distribution in southwestern Ontario, where caves are rare. Pipistrelle sightings in Ontario tend to be concentrated in the Hamilton area, near the Niagara Escarpment, and in eastern Ontario, where there are more caves and mines. As with many other bats, the Eastern Pipistrelle mates in the fall while "swarming" at caves in preparation for hibernation. The sperm is stored in the uterus all winter prior to ovulation in the spring, after which the forty-four-day gestation begins.

EASTERN GRAY SQUIRREL

Everyone is familiar with the Eastern Gray Squirrel, but some people may not realize that the black squirrels we see are the same species, and are simply a different colour morph. Although both colours are found throughout most of the species' range, the black colour morph is more common in northern areas, where the black coat gives the squirrel a thermal advantage — the black fur absorbs more heat.

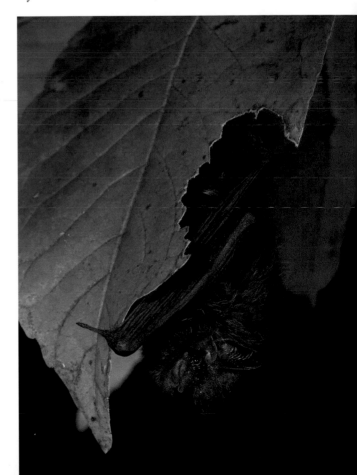

Emerging earlier in the evening than other bats, the Eastern Pipistrelle can be seen flying just before dark in a slow, erratic pattern.

The Eastern Gray Squirrel prefers large stands of mature deciduous forest, but has adapted to the smaller woodlots, residential areas, and urban parks of our fragmented landscape, so long as there remains a predominance of hardwoods. Aside from park handouts and birdfeeder fare, Eastern Gray Squirrels feed on acorns, walnuts, hickory nuts, beech nuts, and other mast. Many of the nuts that squirrels collect are buried for future use, but some are never retrieved. These abandoned seeds help recolonize forest clearings and abandoned fields, propagating future habitat for squirrels and other species of the Carolinian forest.

SOUTHERN FLYING SQUIRREL

Along with the Virginia Opossum, the Southern Flying Squirrel is one of the mammals most often associated with the Carolinian zone. Although it has long been considered a predominately southern species, a recent study found Southern Flying Squirrels north of the French and Mattawa rivers. The same study determined that the northern extent of the range is dependent on winter severity and food supply. With climate warming, we can expect this species to become more common in northern areas.

These nocturnal acrobats have conspicuously large eyes and a loose fold of skin that extends along each side from the wrist of the front foot to the hind foot. When stretched out flat, these folds of skin act like wings, allowing flying squirrels to glide downward from one tree to another over distances of twenty to thirty metres.

WOODLAND VOLE

The Woodland Vole is a small mouse, measuring no more than fourteen centimetres in length, including its very short tail.

Above: Prodigious nut-planters, a single Eastern Gray Squirrel may bury thousands of nuts in one season, digging each into a separate hole, which it then tamps down with its forepaws and nose. There is a great deal of colour variation within this species; some Eastern Gray Squirrels are all black, others have red tails or white tails, but they are all the same species.

Left: The Southern Flying Squirrel does not actually fly but rather glides through the air using a skin membrane that extends from its front foot to hind foot. Dependent on mature forests, Southern Flying Squirrel eats the nuts of mast-producing trees and nests in the cavities of dead standing trees.

Subterranean by nature, it is usually found burrowing in areas of deep sandy soils with a deep humus layer. In Ontario it is primarily restricted to the Norfolk Sand Plain. As a result of this species' dependence on mature Carolinian forests (which tend to have lower temperatures and light conditions and a thicker humus layer on the forest floor than more open woodlands), it has been designated as a species of special concern, and its long-term status in Ontario will depend on our efforts to conserve mature hardwood forests.

Active at night, the Woodland Pine Vole is a secretive mammal that spends most of its time underground.

GRAY FOX

Unlike other members of the dog family, the Gray Fox is quite at home in trees, and often climbs in search of prey, to escape predators, or to find a place to rest. They have an overall grizzled-grey appearance above, with a black stripe extending down the back and onto the tail, and a distinct black patch under each eye.

Although there is a breeding population of Gray Fox on Pelee Island, mainland sightings are scarce and are thought to represent wandering, non-breeding individuals that have recently entered Ontario from the United States. Archaeological excavations show that the Gray Fox was once as common as the Red Fox in Ontario, as far north as Minden, but that it

When winter temperatures are moderate, Badgers emerge from their burrows to hunt for small mammals and rodents.

disappeared in the late seventeenth century, likely just before European settlement, for reasons that are unclear. They reappeared in Ontario in the 1930s, when southern populations expanded their range, but never became as common as they apparently once were. As a result of the limited distribution, the Gray Fox is designated as threatened in Ontario.

BADGER

Few of us will ever be lucky enough to see a Badger in the wild, but those who do will remember the event for life. This amazing predator is designed for subterranean pursuit, with a heavy-set, dorso-ventrally flattened body (flat from back to belly, and wide from side to side) and short, powerful front legs and long claws.

Badgers are mammals of open grasslands, including prairies, pastures, and old fields, where they hunt ground-dwelling prey such as Woodchucks, rabbits, and insects. The flattened body and powerful front legs are adaptations for digging. Rather than chasing down their prey above-ground, Badgers allow their prey to enter the apparent safety of their burrows, and then dig them out.

The main population of Badgers in Ontario is in the Norfolk Sand Plain between Simcoe and Brantford, with a smaller population in the Bothwell Sand Plain between Delaware and London. There have, however, been occasional records as far

west as Kent County and as far north as Grey and Bruce counties. There have also been a few records from the Rainy River area of northwestern Ontario in areas of tallgrass prairie. Unfortunately, almost half of all recent records of Badgers have been of road-killed individuals, a vivid illustration of how fragmentation of our landscape has disastrous consequences for species at risk. The Badger is designated as endangered.

Numbers of White-tailed Deer have expanded significantly in southern Ontario, and this population explosion has taken a huge toll on remaining natural areas, particularly forests. Deer browse on young trees (the browse line is visible in this photo), and have effectively halted regeneration in some woodlands.

MOST MAMMALS IN THE Carolinian zone are relatively common, but for some species, their populations have been reduced and continue to be threatened by loss and fragmentation of their habitat. Species such as Wapiti and Mountain Lion have been lost from the region. Other species, such as Lynx and River Otter, once present in the zone, have all but disappeared from the region, due to habitat loss and degradation, persecution by people, and other factors. The Woodland Vole, Eastern Mole, and Badger, still present in the zone, are all designated as at risk, due, in part, to the ongoing trend of habitat loss. As agricultural practices continue to shift from smaller livestock and family-farm operations to a more industrial cash-crop industry, we will see a continued decline in meadows, pastures, and hedgerows. As this happens, even some of our more common grassland species, such as the Woodchuck, Meadow Jumping Mouse, and Meadow Vole, could be adversely affected.

Although habitat fragmentation is detrimental for many species, it has been beneficial for others. Coyote, Eastern Cottontail, White-tailed Deer, and Raccoon populations have all increased in southern Ontario, because these species thrive in the edge habitat between field and forest, which increases with fragmentation. In the case of White-tailed Deer and Raccoons, populations have increased to the point where they are seriously affecting other plant and animal species. Raccoons eat the eggs and young of ground- and low-nesting bird species, and, with their growing numbers, are now eating up to 95 percent of all turtle nests in some areas. This increased predation can effectively eliminate reproduction of some bird and turtle species.

When deer populations increase above what the landscape can support, there is a serious decline in herbaceous plants and forest regeneration. During the winter, deer eat young tree seedlings and saplings that would replace aging canopy trees. If deer numbers are high enough, regeneration of some tree species is effectively halted, resulting in a potential loss of the forest or a change in forest composition. This situation has occurred in parks such as Rondeau, Point Pelee, and Pinery for many years, but we are now seeing it on a more widespread scale, including in more urban areas such as the Sifton Bog in London. Deer control in a number of these locations has allowed forests to begin the long process of healing.

Although not as colourful or as easy to spot as birds, mammals are an interesting group of animals to study and observe. In the Carolinian zone you can find truly fascinating species, such as the secretive Southern Flying Squirrel, the prehistoric Virginia Opossum, or maybe even the elusive Gray Fox. It is just a matter of looking.

From top to bottom: The Little Brown Bat is the most common bat in Carolinian Canada, often seen at twilight as it swoops and darts in search of insects. It hibernates in caves, hollow trees, and, sometimes, attics. Ubiquitous in urban environments, Raccoons are largely nocturnal, but they make their presence known through tipped-over garbage cans. Their dextrous hands and fingers are capable of turning knobs and lifting latches. When pursued by predators, the Woodland Jumping Mouse hops through the forest like a miniature kangaroo, able to jump more than a metre at a time. This astonishing feat — for such a small creature — is facilitated by its proportionally large hind feet and legs.

CHAPTER 5

CAROLINIAN BIRDS *and* *the* CHANGING NEIGHBOURHOOD

Jon McCracken

Most often seen near rivers and lakes, where prey is abundant, the Bald Eagle feeds on fish and waterfowl. Though still classified as endangered in southern Ontario, this raptor has been making a remarkable recovery around the Great Lakes, thanks to both the ban on the use of DDT in Canada and the U.S. and to the zealous protection of nest sites by proud landowners.

MORE THAN 180 SPECIES of birds nest in the Carolinian zone, making it one of the richest areas for birdlife in Canada. Such an exceptionally high level of diversity results, at least in part, from the fact that the region lies at the intersection of different ecoregions. The Carolinian zone is also blessed with a rich array of habitat types. In addition to large swatches of agricultural and urban lands, the landscape is dotted with numerous marshes and swamps; deciduous, mixed, and coniferous forests; old fields, savannas, and prairies; sandy shorelines and sand spits; and rocky islands. It's a diverse neighbourhood, and there are plenty of niches to fill.

Despite enormous human pressures, only one bird has actually become extinct in this region in the last two hundred years — the Passenger Pigeon. Two species (Wild Turkey and the giant race [a subspecies] of Canada Goose) were formerly extirpated from the region, but were subsequently reintroduced and have flourished. Bald Eagles were nearly wiped out, but have made substantial recovery. Three other species, the Piping

Carolinian Birds 73

Plover, Loggerhead Shrike, and Henslow's Sparrow, may already be extirpated from the Carolinian zone, and face a bleak future across eastern North America.

FAMILIAR BIRDS OF THE CAROLINIAN NEIGHBOURHOOD

Carolinian birds are those species that have the heart of their range lying within the southeastern United States. In Canada, only about thirty species have true Carolinian affinities. The list includes birds with such colourful names as Acadian Flycatcher, Tufted Titmouse, Carolina Wren, Northern Mockingbird, Yellow-breasted Chat, Louisiana Waterthrush, Prothonotary Warbler, White-eyed Vireo, and Orchard Oriole.

Because the Carolinian zone barely extends into southern Canada, our most common birds are more typical of the more temperate Great Lakes–St. Lawrence Forest region. The most common forest-dwelling birds include species that have rather broad geographic ranges: Black-capped Chickadee, Blue Jay, American Crow, Eastern Wood-Pewee, Wood Thrush, Veery, Red-

Top: Ovenbirds are one of the most common birds nesting in the woodlands of Carolinian Canada.

Left: The Eastern Bluebird has made a very strong comeback in Ontario in recent decades, in part due to a popular and successful nest-box program implemented by hundreds of volunteers. Because bluebird populations are very sensitive to harsh winters, this is one species that can be expected to benefit from global warming.

eyed Vireo, Ovenbird, Scarlet Tanager, and Rose-breasted Grosbeak. These are the familiar "bread and butter" woodland birds in southern Ontario, whether you live in Carolinian Canada or the Muskokas.

Without a doubt, the most abundant and ubiquitous forest bird in southern Ontario is the Red-eyed Vireo. Though it spends most of its time high up in the forest canopy and is not readily seen, it advertises its abundance by its incessant singing. Between song bouts, this green-and-white, warbler-like bird hops and flutters along tree branches, methodically checking the undersides of leaves for hidden caterpillars and other insects.

Nearly every Carolinian forest of reasonable size and maturity also hosts Ovenbirds. Like the vireo, this relatively nondescript warbler can be difficult to spot. Unlike the vireo, it spends most of its time on the forest floor, where it builds its peculiar Dutch-oven-shaped nest amongst the leaf litter. Still, the Ovenbird's loud "teacher-teacher-teacher" song is unmistakable and readily gives it away. Unfortunately, Ovenbird populations have declined over much of the species' range, owing to forest loss and fragmentation. Once common, it is now almost gone from Essex County.

Another rather drab and nondescript woodland bird is the Eastern Wood-Pewee. But it, too, is a conspicuous songster, whistling its plaintive, querying "pee-a-weeee" song. The pewee

The American Kestrel hunts for grasshoppers, mice, and small birds over roadsides, pastures, grasslands, and open savannas. In such habitats, pairs will readily occupy nest boxes that are installed high up on telephone poles.

With its bright red colour, the male Scarlet Tanager is one of the most colourful birds in the Carolinian region.

is a type of flycatcher. Scanning the nearby airspace for prey, it sits motionless on a branch, and then darts out to snatch small flying insects, with an audible snap of its beak.

Like an ice-cream sandwich, the upper parts of the Wood Thrush are a rich chocolate brown, and its vanilla-white breast appears to be liberally sprinkled with dark chocolate chips. Spending much of its time on or near the ground, it blends in well with the forest floor. Anyone taking an early summer's walk in the Carolinian forest in the misty sunrise will be enchanted by the Wood Thrush's flute-like, ethereal, liquid song. Though it is still common, Wood Thrush populations have declined across much of eastern North America, owing to the loss, fragmentation, and degradation of mature forest habitats.

Of course, there are many birds with much flashier plumage in the forest. Take the tanagers, for example. In Ontario, we are fortunate to have the Scarlet Tanager. Although common and brightly coloured, the Scarlet Tanager can be remarkably difficult to spot against a backdrop of green foliage. But should you catch a glimpse of a brilliant male lit up in a patch of blazing sunlight, you may well find yourself dazzled.

Nearly every woodland in Carolinian Canada also supports good numbers of Rose-breasted Grosbeaks. The male grosbeak's black-and-white pattern gives it a distinguished formal look, while its rosy-red vest seems to add a stamp of refined nobility. Grosbeaks eat plenty of insects, but their large, imposing bills are also powerful enough to split open even the toughest seeds, making them important seed-dispersal agents.

THE CAROLINIAN NEIGHBOURHOOD EXPANDS

A century ago, our grandparents or great-grandparents would have been astonished to see a number of Carolinian birds that we now take for granted. Indeed, one of the most interesting trends in North American ornithology over the past hundred years is the northward range expansion of so many species from the United States into southern Ontario. These northern shifts are completely in keeping with what is predicted by global warming. In addition, ongoing loss of natural habitats south of the border has likely created habitat-supply bottlenecks that effectively "squeeze" many kinds of southern birds northward into Canada.

There are numerous examples. One of the best is the Northern Cardinal, which was simply not seen in the neighbourhood in 1900. Since then, it has happily settled into all of southern Ontario, its presence likely encouraged by more moderate

Below: Contrary to popular belief, not all waterfowl are associated with marshes. For example, the Hooded Merganser (pictured below) and the Wood Duck nest in tree cavities in swamp forests and along the wooded borders of slow-moving streams and rivers.

Bottom: The Carolinian region is recognized internationally for its rich and varied bird life. During spring migration, birdwatchers flock to the zone to see species such as the Tundra Swan, which uses flooded fields full of crop residues as "staging" areas on its journey north.

winters and the proliferation of bird feeders.

Even more amazing is the northward expansion of the Mourning Dove, which also began about a hundred years ago. Taking advantage of human changes in the environment (bird feeders, waste grain in farmers' fields, planting of ornamental conifers, warmer winters as a result of climate change), the Mourning Dove is now exceptionally abundant across southern and central Ontario — and is extending its range into the boreal forest.

Another example is the Turkey Vulture, a species entirely absent from Ontario in 1900. It is now a common sight across the southern and central parts of the province, and it too has been

Above: With the growing number of bird feeders, the unmistakable Northern Cardinal has become a welcome and familiar sight across southern Ontario. Feeding stations help non-migratory, southern species such as the cardinal, Mourning Dove, Tufted Titmouse, Northern Mockingbird, and Red-bellied Woodpecker survive our northern winters.

Left: Unlike nearly all other birds, the Turkey Vulture has a well-developed sense of smell, which it uses (along with its keen eyesight) to help locate carrion. The Turkey Vulture is a true master of the wind, capable of sailing effortlessly for long distances with hardly a flap of its massive wings.

extending its range even farther northward into the boreal forest region. A variety of reasons have been offered to explain its remarkable range expansion. Chief among them is the development of the road network, along with a burgeoning deer population, which supplies a constant source of carrion. Another reason is a more moderate climate.

Once driven almost to extinction by market hunters who sold its feathers for the millinery trade, the Great Egret, too, was formerly not found in Ontario. Though still quite patchily distributed in the Carolinian zone, this strikingly majestic bird is now a common sight in large marshes in extreme southwestern Ontario, especially in Essex County.

The tiny Blue-gray Gnatcatcher is not much bigger than a hummingbird. These nervous little birds seem to move non-stop through the forest canopy, pointing their long tails straight up like exclamation points, and occasionally wheezing out a pitiful, nasal call note. Their tiny jewel-like nest is constructed of thousands of flecks of lichen, which are painstakingly woven together with spider webs. Though nowhere common, gnatcatchers are now widespread, and their populations have increased significantly in the Carolinian zone in the past half-century.

Another new addition to the Carolinian zone's avifauna is the Northern Mockingbird. Boldly patterned with splotches of grey, black, and white, the mockingbird seems to do well in many human-modified landscapes. It is renowned for its remarkable ability to faithfully mimic the songs of other birds. Even world-class birdwatchers can be easily fooled by a mockingbird's renditions. Its population has increased exponentially in the last couple of decades, especially in the Niagara, Hamilton, and Toronto regions.

The colourful Red-shouldered Hawk requires expansive tracts of relatively undisturbed, older-growth swamp forest — few of which now remain in southwestern Ontario. Along with small mammals and forest birds, its rather specialized diet includes frogs and snakes, many of which are also in serious decline.

THE NEIGHBOURHOOD RETREATS: SPECIES AT RISK

While the diversity of breeding birds in Carolinian Canada has been enhanced by the welcome addition of new species that have immigrated here over the last century, the populations of some other Carolinian species are so small and precarious, and they have such specialized habitat needs, that they are at risk of extirpation.

The colourful Red-shouldered Hawk, for example, was once the most common hawk in southern Ontario, but it has almost entirely disappeared from the Carolinian zone, owing to habitat

Top: The Acadian Flycatcher is a migratory songbird that nests in older growth forests, one of the region's most threatened habitats.

Above: The Barn Owl nests in barns, silos, abandoned houses, and standing dead trees. These nocturnal hunters are efficient predators, flying over grasslands and farm fields in search of meadow voles, mice, and rats.

loss and degradation. The Red-shouldered Hawk prefers quiet, swampy areas in large, older-growth forests for nesting. Snakes and frogs, many of which are also in decline, are favourite foods.

Formerly abundant at the time of European settlement, the Northern Bobwhite is now nearly extirpated from the Carolinian zone, owing to loss of grassland habitats and unrestricted hunting and trapping by settlers. A healthy population still persists only in the Walpole Island First Nation territory at Lake St. Clair. Other than the Walpole Island bobwhite population, most (if not all) bobwhites seen in Ontario are non-native, farm-reared birds that have been released for hunting or have escaped captivity. These released birds rarely survive more than a few months.

The Barn Owl is nearly extirpated from the Carolinian zone. Never a common species in Ontario, its population has experienced significant declines across the entire North American continent, again stemming from the tremendous loss of grassland habitats.

Now endangered, the King Rail was formerly much more common and widespread across its North American range. In the Carolinian zone, it is now primarily restricted to large, diverse marshes along Lake St. Clair and Lake Erie, where fewer than one hundred pairs remain. Loss and degradation of wetlands are the most significant threats to its survival.

With a population of no more than about fifty pairs, the Acadian Flycatcher is designated as endangered in Canada. Small, inconspicuous, and olive-green, it can be found only by listening carefully for its emphatic "peeetsa" song. The Acadian

Flycatcher requires very special conservation attention, since it needs blocks of old-growth forest, especially in ravines and swamps. Because these types of woodland do not have a thick understorey layer, they provide the kind of uncluttered, open-air space that this flycatcher needs for foraging.

You'll need to strain your neck to find the sky-blue Cerulean Warbler singing his buzzy song way up high in a towering Tulip-tree or oak. Though the heart of this warbler's range lies within the United States, southern Ontario's breeding population is increasingly important to the continued survival of this severely declining species. The Cerulean Warbler requires large continuous tracts of very mature deciduous forest, either in dry-upland or wet, swampy situations. By spending the entire breeding season in the upper reaches of the tree canopy, the Cerulean Warbler occupies a specialized niche in the forest and avoids competitive interactions with other species.

The Prothonotary Warbler, one of Canada's rarest birds, is a small songbird that nests in cavities of rotting trees in rich swamp forests. Distinctive features include its relatively long bill, bright yellow head, and slate-blue wings.

With fewer than twenty pairs of Prothonotary Warblers now in all of Canada, the species is critically endangered. Its population has been declining steadily throughout eastern North America, owing to the loss of forested wetlands in both its breeding and wintering grounds. In Canada, it is now almost entirely restricted to swamp forests bordering Lake Erie. Much sought after by birders for its exceptional beauty and tameness, the Prothonotary Warbler is the only warbler species in eastern North America that nests in tree cavities. It also readily occupies nest boxes.

To Canadian birders, the Hooded Warbler is probably regarded as the quintessential Carolinian species. Its yellow-and-green body is strikingly offset by a jet-black hood. Though it is still regarded as threatened in Canada, the good news is that this species has experienced a dramatic population expansion recently, especially in maturing woodlands of Elgin, Norfolk, and Niagara regions. Hooded Warblers nest in dense shrubby tangles that proliferate after small gaps are created beneath a mature forest canopy. Thanks to the stewardship of many private and public landowners, the Hooded Warbler is benefiting from the maturation of second-growth forest in the Carolinian zone, coupled with judicious logging practices that retain a sizeable proportion of older trees.

Top: Once extirpated as a nesting species from this region, the reintroduction of the Canada Goose ranks among the most amazing conservation success stories in the world. Within only a scant three decades of the first releases, the Canada Goose is now so abundant and widespread that it is considered a nuisance by many farmers and urbanites.

Left: Every spring, Tundra Swans embark on a three-month-long migration from the U.S. Atlantic coast to the high Canadian Arctic, a 3,000-km journey that takes them through the Carolinian zone. They often congregate at Pinery Provincial Park, where as many as 10,000 swans can be seen at one time if conditions are favourable.

The Neighbourhood Makes a Comeback

While conservation challenges in the Carolinian zone are significant, they are by no means unsurpassable. Species and habitats can be recovered, and a few of the most remarkable success stories can serve as inspiration.

The Canada Goose is one excellent case study. It is difficult to imagine that the "giant" race (subspecies) of the Canada Goose was actually thought to be extinct until the mid-1950s, when a small remnant population was discovered nesting in the United States. Massive captive-breeding and reintroduction programs were subsequently implemented across its former range. While costly, these programs have been so phenomenally successful that giant Canada Geese are now regarded as nuisance birds in many agricultural and urban areas.

Like so many other game birds, Wood Duck populations across North America were threatened by unrestricted market hunting in the 1800s. With the introduction of protective laws in the early 1900s, this species made a dramatic comeback, and it is now once again abundant in the Carolinian zone.

Wild Turkeys were once a staple food item for European settlers in southern Ontario. The species disappeared entirely from the province by the late 1800s, due to over hunting and loss

The Wild Turkey was common in southern Ontario forests at the time of European settlement, but was extirpated in the late 1800s because of forest habitat loss and unrestricted hunting. It is now once again common here, thanks to reforestation efforts, along with a very successful reintroduction program.

The Black Tern nests in small colonies in expanses of marshes with large patches of open water. It is experiencing population declines in parts of its range, likely due to habitat loss and degradation, and is among several species of conservation concern in the Carolinian region.

of forest habitat. In the 1980s, a program was launched to reintroduce Wild Turkeys in Ontario, using wild stock obtained from several U.S. states. Within only two decades, turkeys have become common once more in Carolinian Canada and across their former range. The success of the reintroduction program would not have been possible had it not been for the efforts of private landowners and public land managers to protect and recover forested habitat in southern Ontario.

THE FUTURE OF THE NEIGHBOURHOOD

We will likely continue to welcome more bird species into Canada's Carolinian zone, particularly if climate-change predictions are borne out. Among the expected new arrivals are the Black Vulture, Summer Tanager, Blue Grosbeak, and Worm-eating Warbler. At the same time, we can also expect to lose some species because of habitat loss and degradation.

Grassland birds seem to be most at risk in the region. For some, like the Northern Bobwhite, Barn Owl, Short-eared Owl, and Henslow's Sparrow, there is currently little hope for recovery within this region. If long-term trends continue, even common grassland birds, like the Bobolink, Eastern Meadowlark, and Vesper Sparrow, could be added to the list of species at risk in the not-too-distant future.

Meanwhile, several species of marsh birds continue to decline. Without strong, proactive recovery efforts, the King Rail, Least Bittern, and Black Tern will face significant challenges.

There is also increasing concern about the mysterious widespread declines that are occurring amongst many of the aerial foraging species – notably swallows, martins, swifts, Whip-poor-wills, and Common Nighthawks. And then there are the forest birds, like the Prothonotary Warbler, the Acadian Flycatcher, and the Louisiana Waterthrush, which are barely hanging on in Ontario.

Recovery teams have been established to benefit several species at risk by working through detailed recovery strategies and action plans. Across Carolinian Canada, landowners and citizen volunteers are increasingly engaged at all levels. Their involvement and commitment are truly fundamental to species recovery. Skilled volunteers provide an essential role by helping to track bird population trends through a wide range of coordinated monitoring programs. More and more private landowners are proudly incorporating natural-heritage features and "best management practices" across the rural countryside. Naturalist groups, Conservation Authorities, and other

Top: The Brown-headed Cowbird, a western species that has dramatically expanded its breeding range eastwards, parasitizes the nests of songbirds, reducing nest productivity of the host. Pictured here are three blue eggs of the Veery (a kind of forest-dwelling thrush) and a cowbird egg.

Above: The Louisiana Waterthrush is one of Carolinian Canada's rarest birds, restricted to large expanses of mature swamp and to the forested borders of coldwater streams that pass through ravines. It hides its nest very cleverly in mossy crevices in stream banks and stumps.

In advance of their fall migration, Red-winged Blackbirds start to gather in flocks to feast on Wild Rice in the relatively few pristine marshes that remain in Carolinian Canada. With the dramatic loss of wetland habitat, the blackbirds now take advantage of corn and grain crops, much to the consternation of farmers.

environmental agencies are actively working together to restore wetlands, prairies, savannas, and the Carolinian forest.

By far the easiest thing one can do to help these species not only hang on but thrive is to preserve and nurture existing natural areas. The best spots to find the Carolinian zone's speciality bird species are well known, and these are the most important areas to protect and enhance. Places like Backus Woods, Rondeau Provincial Park, Skunk's Misery, Dundas Valley, St. Williams Conservation Reserve, South Walsingham Sand Ridges, Spooky Hollow, Turkey Point, Holiday Beach, Point Abino, Walpole Island, Fonthill Kame, Lambton County Heritage Forest, Point Pelee, and the vast marshes of Long Point and Lake St. Clair are just some of the sites that have exceptional national importance, and have been designated as globally Important Bird Areas (IBAs). Many of these sites have received, and must continue to receive, considerable conservation attention. After all, it is because of these key places that many Carolinian birds are able to persist in Canada.

CHAPTER 6

THE HIDDEN WORLD *of* AMPHIBIANS *and* REPTILES

Michael J. Oldham

The distinctive mating call of a Fowler's Toad, a sheep-like bleat or wail, can be heard in May along beaches on the north shore of Lake Erie. Fowler's Toad looks similar to the more common American Toad, but many of its dark brown spots contain three or more warts.

CAROLINIAN CANADA IS HOME to the greatest diversity of amphibians and reptiles in Canada. They are found in most Carolinian habitats, except those most heavily modified by humans. Because they are often small, secretive, and rare, many Carolinian amphibians and reptiles are infrequently seen and poorly known to the general public.

Amphibians and reptiles are often grouped together, and referred to collectively as herptiles or herps, but they are in fact very different and not closely related. Amphibians generally have a smooth, moist skin, lay their eggs in water, and pass

Top: The Eastern Red-backed Salamander is Ontario's most common salamander. Unlike most amphibians, which lay their eggs in water, the Eastern Red-backed Salamander usually lays them inside rotten logs.

Above: Although widespread in Carolinian Canada, the Spotted Salamander is seldom seen because it spends most of its life underground.

through an aquatic larval stage (such as the familiar tadpole stage of frogs and toads). Reptiles have dry, scaly skin, and lay their eggs on land or, in the case of some lizard and snake species, give birth to live young. They do not have an aquatic larval stage.

Herptiles are ectothermic (or cold-blooded), meaning that they cannot generate heat internally like birds and mammals do, and are dependent on their surroundings for warmth. As a result, amphibians and reptiles are much more abundant and diverse in warmer climates; indeed, most Carolinian species are at the northern limit of their range. In winter, most Ontario amphibians and reptiles hibernate.

Because Carolinian Canada is one of the warmest parts of the country and has a great diversity of habitats, it supports the greatest herp diversity — a total of fifty-one species. Of the twenty-four amphibian species in the region, twelve are salamanders and twelve are frogs or toads. Of the twenty-seven reptile species, ten are turtles, sixteen are snakes, and one is a lizard. Three species formerly known from the region are now extirpated — the Eastern Tiger Salamander, the Northern Spring Salamander, and the Timber Rattlesnake.

SALAMANDERS AND NEWTS

Ontario's salamanders are generally small and secretive, spending much of their lives either underground, underwater, or beneath logs, rocks, or other types of cover. Most live in woodlands, where they can be quite common. One study demonstrated that the biomass of woodland salamanders in a New England forest is higher than that of breeding birds.

Most Ontario salamanders lay their eggs in woodland ponds, though the terrestrial Eastern Red-backed Salamander lays its eggs in moist, decaying logs. One Ontario salamander, the Common Mudpuppy, is entirely aquatic, living in the Great Lakes and in some streams, rivers, and lakes.

Of the Carolinian zone's twelve salamanders, two are extirpated, and three others are endangered or threatened. The Eastern Tiger Salamander is known in Canada only from a single Canadian record taken in 1915 at Point Pelee. The Northern Spring Salamander, while still present in southern Quebec, is known in Ontario only from an 1877 specimen from the Niagara Region. Two species of dusky salamander occur in the Niagara River Gorge and nowhere else in the province, though both also occur in southern Quebec. Until 1989, when it was found in a couple of small streams and seepages, the Northern Dusky Salamander was thought to be extirpated from the province. Only in 2004 did biologists realize that some of the dusky salamanders at these sites in Niagara were actually a separate, but closely related, species, the Allegheny Mountain Dusky Salamander. These two species are so similar that their identification could only be confirmed by genetic testing, which was carried out by scientists at McGill University in Montreal.

Five members of the mole salamander genus, *Ambystoma*, are known from the Carolinian zone, one of which is the extirpated Eastern Tiger Salamander. Mole salamanders are so named

The Red-spotted Newt, a subspecies of the Eastern Newt, has a complex life cycle: it spends most of its life in water but does spend one stage on land as well. Its diet includes insects, worms, molluscs, and crustaceans.

The American Bullfrog, the largest frog in North America, prefers large bodies of water, and is most commonly found hiding in the vegetation along the water's edge. It emits a vibrant call from an inflated pouch under its chin.

because they spend most of their lives underground, emerging primarily in the spring to mate and lay their eggs in vernal woodland ponds. Vernal ponds are created in spring by snow melt and spring rains, have no fish, and usually contain water until late summer or fall, allowing salamander larvae sufficient time to metamorphose before the pond dries up or freezes.

Ontario has one species of newt, the Eastern Newt, with the Red-spotted Newt subspecies inhabiting the Carolinian zone. The Eastern Newt life cycle differs from that of other Ontario salamanders, since there is a terrestrial juvenile stage — the bright orange red-eft stage — between the aquatic larval stage and aquatic adult stage. Adult newts are found in artificial and natural ponds, while the red-eft stage occurs in woodlands. Efts are thought to be brightly coloured to warn potential predators of their toxic skin secretions.

FROGS AND TOADS

Frogs and toads are a common sight in most Ontario wetlands, and many rural residents are familiar with their distinctive spring and summer breeding calls. All Ontario species depend

on bodies of water for egg-laying and larval development. Some of our larger species, such as the American Bullfrog, require permanent bodies of water, since their larvae (tadpoles) spend several years in the water before metamorphosing. Tadpoles of other species transform during the same year the eggs are laid, meaning that these species can breed in temporary bodies of water, where fish predators are absent. Frogs and toads are very similar, although toads are more terrestrial and generally wander farther away from water. The thick, warty skin of toads does not cause warts, but does protect the animal from drying out, allowing it to live in drier habitats than most frogs.

The camouflage of the Gray Treefrog makes it difficult to spot when it is clinging to the bark of trees. Its call, a musical trill, is distinctive though sometimes mistaken for a bird call since it is often heard from tree tops on warm, humid summer days.

Carolinian Canada's twelve frog and toad species consist of two toads (Bufonidae family), four members of the treefrog family (Hylidae), and six true frogs (Ranidae). Unlike Ontario's other amphibian and reptile groups, most frogs and toads found in Carolinian Canada are not at risk; only two are officially designated as species at risk. Fowler's Toad, restricted to sandy areas on the north shore of Lake Erie, is a provincially and nationally threatened species. Blanchard's Cricket Frog was last confirmed in Canada on Pelee Island in the 1970s, and is now probably extirpated. Even though not listed as at risk in Ontario, several common amphibians, such as the Northern Leopard Frog and Western Chorus Frog, are declining in parts of their Canadian range and warrant careful monitoring in the Carolinian zone.

TURTLES

Turtles are an ancient group and have survived on earth virtually unchanged for millions of years. Most Ontario species spend their lives in or near water. Many turtles bask on rocks or logs in order to raise their body temperatures. All turtle species lay soft-shelled eggs on land, usually burying them in sand, gravel, or loose soil near a wetland. Hatchling turtles emerge in late summer, or sometimes hatch and spend their first winter in the nest cavity, emerging the following spring.

Turtles are more threatened than any other herp group, with 67 percent of native turtle species in Carolinian Canada listed as species at risk. Only two

Spotted Turtles lay their eggs in small flask-shaped nests in shallow, soft-bottomed wetlands such as marshes, bogs, swamps, and ponds. Their sex is determined by the temperature during incubation — cooler temperatures produce more males and warmer temperatures produce more females.

Top: With its pancake-like rubbery shell, the Spiny Softshell is swift on land and in water. Its long neck and tubular snout allow it to breathe while hiding underwater by stretching its nose to the surface like a snorkel.

Above: Blanding's Turtle is a large turtle with a high, domed shell and a bright lemon-yellow throat. Ontario has a larger portion of the global range of this species than any other jurisdiction.

of nine native turtle species in the Carolinian zone are relatively widespread and secure: the Snapping Turtle, Canada's largest non-marine turtle, and the familiar Painted Turtle. However, even these two species have declined in some areas.

Turtles frequently have to cross roads to reach their nesting sites, and at their slow pace they are extremely vulnerable while travelling these dangerous routes. Some females even choose to nest on road shoulders, where they and their hatchlings are often killed by vehicles. A variety of mammals such as Raccoons, Striped Skunks, Red Foxes, Virginia Opossums, and Coyotes also raid their nests, destroying eggs. Some of these predators exist at unnaturally high levels in the Carolinian region due to an abundance of human-related foods, such as garbage and agricultural crops. Yet another serious threat to some turtle species is commercial collection for the pet trade, which can decimate turtle populations. Because many species of turtles reach maturity at a late age and have a low ratio of egg-to-adult survival, removal of a few reproductive adults can permanently damage populations.

LIZARDS

Lizards are a common and conspicuous animal group in deserts and tropical areas, but few species range as far north as Canada. Lizards and snakes are closely related, being grouped together in the order Squamata. It is thought that snakes evolved from a lizard-like ancestor.

Eastern Canada's only lizard species, the Common Five-lined Skink, is a rare inhabitant of the Carolinian zone. This small lizard occurs in two separate areas of the province; it is known from a few sites in extreme southwestern Ontario and along the southern edge of the Precambrian Shield from southern Georgian Bay to the St. Lawrence River. In the Carolinian zone, skinks inhabit a few isolated natural areas, such as Rondeau and Pinery parks, and Point Pelee, where they are vulnerable to habitat loss (such as removal of logs and other cover items from beaches) and collection for the pet trade. The protection offered by provincial and national parks is important to survival in such areas, as is stewardship of private woodlots and wetlands.

SNAKES

Although some herp groups are well liked by the public (for example, turtles), snakes are, in general, greatly feared and misunderstood, and some snakes are still killed by a small proportion of the human

Below: Turtle nests are vulnerable to predation from a variety of animals, including skunks and Raccoons.

Bottom: The Common Five-lined Skink can be found in rotting stumps and logs, and in damp, decaying debris in woodlands. Its striped pattern becomes less conspicuous as it grows larger, and its bright blue tail often turns grey as it ages.

The entire world distribution of the endangered Lake Erie Watersnake is restricted to the islands of western Lake Erie and a portion of the Catawba/Marblehead Peninsula in Ohio.

population. This fear is largely unfounded, since only one snake found in the Carolinian region, the Eastern Massasauga, is venomous, and it has a very restricted distribution and is not large or aggressive.

In Ontario, all snakes hibernate, sometimes communally with other individuals of the same or different species, in other cases singly. All snakes are carnivorous and swallow their food whole.

Snakes are the most diverse group of Carolinian herps, with sixteen species, one of which has two subspecies. Only one of these species, the Eastern Gartersnake, is common and conspicuous. It is also Canada's most widespread reptile species, and ranges from coast to coast and north to the Arctic Circle, the only Canadian reptile to live this far north. In the Carolinian zone, there is an unusual all-black (melanistic) colour form of the Eastern Gartersnake, primarily on Lake Erie peninsulas and islands. It is thought that these darker snakes have a thermal advantage over normally coloured Eastern Gartersnakes, allowing them to warm up more quickly in the spring, which outweighs their greater visibility and vulnerability to predators. Two relatives of the Eastern Gartersnake that appear similar also live in the Carolinian zone: the prairie-inhabiting Butler's Gartersnake and the more aquatic Northern Ribbonsnake.

There are three types of watersnake in the Carolinian region: the rare and specialized Queen Snake, the Northern Watersnake, and the Lake Erie Watersnake. Queen Snakes are restricted to a few rivers, streams, and marshes, where they are secretive and poorly known. Their specialized diet of newly moulted crayfish means that Queen Snakes are dependent on good water quality. Northern Watersnakes are widespread in southern and central Ontario, though rare in much of the Carolinian zone, while Lake Erie Watersnakes have the most restricted global range of any Canadian herp, living only on a few islands in western Lake Erie. Watersnakes feed primarily on fish, and in recent years the diet of the Lake Erie Watersnake has switched almost exclusively to the introduced Round Goby. Round Gobies in Lake Erie feed largely on another introduced species, the Zebra Mussel (and the related Quagga Mussel, also introduced). There is concern that filter-feeding Zebra Mussels are accumulating environmental contaminants from polluted Lake Erie waters and passing these contaminants up the food chain to Round Gobies and then to Lake Erie Watersnakes; through biomagnification — the concentration of toxins as they move up the food chain — these toxic chemicals may be adversely affecting the endangered Lake Erie Watersnake.

Canada's largest snake, the Eastern Ratsnake, reaches a length of more than two metres, and is a rare inhabitant of the Carolinian zone. It lives in a few regions with a higher percentage of forest cover, such as the Skunk's Misery area and parts of the Norfolk Sand Plain. A related species, the Eastern Foxsnake, has a large portion of its small global range in Ontario and is a high conservation priority for the province. Both these species and the slightly more common Eastern Milksnake are constrictors, and feed on a variety of animals, including frogs, other snakes, mammals, and birds. Contrary to popular belief, constricting snakes do not crush their prey to death, but suffocate their prey by gradually tightening their coils until the unfortunate victim can no longer breathe. Constricting snakes in the Carolinian zone, due to their small size, pose no threat to humans.

Historically, two venomous snakes inhabited the Carolinian zone, but, as humans settled the region, these snakes were directly persecuted and their habitats were destroyed and degraded. The larger Timber Rattlesnake was extirpated from Canada by the 1950s. The smaller Massasauga (rarely reaching one metre in length) has fared slightly better, though its survival in the Carolinian zone is precarious. At one time Eastern Massasaugas were widespread in the region, but they now persist in only two small areas, Ojibway Prairie in Windsor and the Wainfleet Bog in

Above: The Eastern Massasauga, Ontario's only extant venomous snake, is not aggressive, and shies away from human contact. This threatened rattlesnake is found in small numbers in only two places in Carolinian Canada — Wainfleet Bog and Ojibway Prairie Complex.

Below: Wary and shy, and seldom found more than a few metres from a permanent body of water, the aquatic Queen Snake sometimes basks on shrubs overhanging rivers and creeks, dropping into the water at the first sign of danger.

Habitats occupied by the Eastern Foxsnake include oak savannas, prairies, and lakeside marshes. This is Ontario's second-largest snake, after the Eastern Ratsnake, reaching two metres in length.

the Niagara Peninsula. The Eastern Massasauga Recovery Team is making intensive efforts to reverse this trend, so that this unique animal will survive among Canada's fauna.

CONSERVATION AND RECOVERY

Global amphibian declines have received a lot of attention in recent years. One-third of Carolinian amphibian species are listed as species at risk, while two-thirds of reptile species are considered at risk. The primary cause is the same problem facing almost all native Carolinian species: habitat loss. Many herptiles live in wetlands for at least part of their lives, and these areas have been especially hard hit by habitat loss and degradation. Amphibians in particular, with their porous skin and greater dependency on aquatic habitats, are vulnerable to a variety of pollutants, and are thought to have declined in many areas due to exposure to toxic chemicals. Habitat fragmentation is another major threat, since many species migrate from upland habitats to wetlands for breeding and hibernation. Likewise, vehicular traffic is a serious and increasing threat. As the number of roads and traffic volume increase, many amphibians and reptiles are killed as they cross roads.

Exotic invasive species are a serious conservation issue in Carolinian Canada, but only one reptile, the Red-eared Slider, a

turtle commonly sold in pet stores, is definitely an exotic species that has established itself in the wild in the region, where it may be a threat to native turtle populations, through disease transmission, for example. The Eastern Box Turtle is thought to have been originally native to the Carolinian region, since its remains have been found in a number of archaeological sites; however, recent Ontario Eastern Box Turtle sightings are most likely the result of the release of captive animals by pet owners.

Recovery teams have been set up for most of Carolinian Canada's at-risk herptiles. These teams are made up of experts and others involved with the conservation of the species, including academics, students, government biologists, and interested naturalists and landowners, and are involved in a variety of monitoring, research, captive propagation, and education programs. The recovery of many of the Carolinian zone's rarer amphibians and reptiles will be difficult and can only be accomplished through the cooperation of government agencies, landowners, and the public.

ALTHOUGH FAR LESS CONSPICUOUS and well known than many Carolinian-zone animals, amphibians and reptiles are

Rocky shorelines along Middle Island, in western Lake Erie, provide prime habitat for the endangered Lake Erie Watersnake. The snake hunts for small fish and crayfish in the water along shorelines.

The Eastern Foxsnake is one of Ontario's egg-laying snake species (approximately half of the province's snake species give birth to live young, the other lay eggs). Their eggs have a rubbery, pliable shell, unlike the hard-shelled eggs of birds.

abundant and diverse in healthy ecosystems. Widespread declines of many species are an indication of environmental degradation. Interested naturalists can contribute to the conservation of Carolinian herps by participating in one or more of the monitoring programs coordinated by Bird Studies Canada, Environment Canada, and the Toronto Zoo, or by submitting records to the provincial amphibian and reptile atlas coordinated by the Ontario Natural Heritage Information Centre. Increased conservation attention is required so that future generations can enjoy these fascinating creatures.

CHAPTER 7

BELOW *the* WATER'S SURFACE: FISHES *and* FRESHWATER MUSSELS

Shawn Staton and Alan Dextrase

WHILE THE MORE CHARISMATIC terrestrial flora and fauna of Carolinian Canada tend to attract the most attention, the wetlands, streams, rivers, and lakes of the zone harbour a parallel world of hidden treasures. Indeed, the waters of the region support a diversity of freshwater life, including some of the area's most unusual species. Fishes, freshwater mussels, crayfish, and the nymphs of dragonflies, damselflies, mayflies, and stoneflies, as well as a host of other invertebrates and plants, comprise these freshwater communities. This chapter focuses on two of the larger and better-known groups: the fishes and the freshwater mussels.

The watersheds of Carolinian Canada support the richest communities of fishes and freshwater mussels in the country.

The Sydenham River has more freshwater mussel species (thirty-four) than any other river in Canada. The only major watershed that lies completely within the Carolinian region, the Sydenham River supports the healthiest remaining Canadian populations of several globally rare species.

The Northern Riffleshell is a small, colourful freshwater mussel that lives in highly oxygenated riffles of rivers and streams. The Sydenham River population of this rare mussel is one of only four reproducing populations that remain globally.

More than half of the 230 species of fishes known to exist in Canada can be found in the region; 93 fish species have been reported from the Thames River alone. Similarly, 34 species of freshwater mussels (about two-thirds of the mussel species found in Canada) live in the Sydenham River, the only major river system that falls entirely within the Carolinian zone.

The waterways of the region also include a high proportion of Canada's species at risk, some of which, such as the Rayed Bean and Northern Madtom, are globally rare and threatened with extinction.

The diverse communities of fishes and mussels in the region can be attributed primarily to climate and biogeography. Southern Ontario enjoys some of the mildest climatic conditions in the country, and thus many species survive here at the northern limit of their range. As well, Carolinian Canada occurs in the lower Great Lakes watershed, which is closest to — and had numerous connections with — the species-rich glacial refuge (ice-free area) in the Mississippi Valley. When the glaciers receded, thousands of years ago, high numbers of species re-invaded Carolinian waterways from this refuge, which was the centre of evolution for fishes and mussels in North America.

FRESHWATER MUSSELS

Almost everyone has encountered the shells of native freshwater mussels, or "clams," along the shores of rivers and lakes, but few people are aware of the incredible diversity of mussels that occurs in the Carolinian region. The variety in shape, size, colour, and reproductive biology of the numerous species is fascinating, and comes as a complete surprise even to many well-rounded naturalists and biologists.

Mussel species in the region range in size from the tiny Rayed Bean (as small as a lima bean) all the way up to the White Heel-splitter, which can reach the size of a dinner plate. Their shells range in colour from the rather unassuming plain brown of the Salamander Mussel to the strikingly beautiful rayed patterns of species like the Northern Riffleshell and the Wavyrayed Lampmussel. On the inside of the shell is the smooth, pearly surface called the "nacre," which can vary in colour from the

more common white to pink, salmon, or the dark purple nacre found in species such as the Spike. Some species like the Paper Pondshell have very thin shells, whereas others, such as the Mucket, have much heavier shells, often exceeding one centimetre in thickness. Decades ago, some of these heavier-shelled species were even harvested commercially for the pearl-button industry. In the United States, mussel shells are still harvested for use in the cultured-pearl industry (beads cut from the shells are used as "seed pearls"). The intriguing names of many species often reflect the characteristics of their shell form, with the Purple Wartyback, Round Pigtoe, Mapleleaf, and Snuffbox providing good examples. Likewise, the Pimpleback gets its name from the distinctive, irregular pustules, or "pimples," on its shell.

Freshwater mussels are filter feeders. They filter their microscopic food from the water and, in doing so, contribute to water clarity. Individual mussels can filter up to twenty litres of water per day. It is therefore no surprise that a dense "bed" of mussels can contribute substantially to improving water quality. Preferred habitats for mussels can vary from the sand or muck bottoms of lakes to the gravelly bottoms of swifter rivers and streams. Many species, such as the Northern Riffleshell, prefer well-aerated areas called "riffles," in larger rivers and streams.

Top: The Pimpleback is easily distinguished from other mussels by its rotund form and the presence of irregular pustules or "pimples" on its shell. Smaller juveniles sometimes lack pustules, but typically have a distinctive, wide, greenish-blue ray.

Above: The Black Sandshell is one of the largest freshwater mussels found in the Carolinian region, sometimes approaching twenty centimetres in length.

The Rayed Bean is one of the Carolinian zone's smallest freshwater mussels, reaching a total length of less than four centimetres. Although once more widespread in the region, it is now restricted mainly to the Sydenham River.

Here, they embed themselves in the gravel, and filter their food from the water as it passes by.

Freshwater mussels have a surprisingly complex and unique reproductive cycle. All species are parasitic on fish during their early life stage, with the exception of the Salamander Mussel, which is parasitic on the Mudpuppy, an aquatic salamander. Fertilization occurs when male mussels release sperm into the water, and the sperm are filtered out by nearby females. Brooding females later release larvae, called glochidia, which attach themselves to the gills or fins of the host fish species (or, in the case of the Salamander Mussel, to the host Mudpuppy). After a few months to a year, the "hitch-hiking" glochidia drop off the host as tiny juvenile mussels to complete their life cycle as free-living adults. Since adult mussels move very little, the host relationship provides the added advantage of a dispersal mechanism for the young mussels, allowing them to colonize new areas.

The fascinating parasite-host relationship that all mussel species have is often highly specific. For example, the Wavyrayed Lampmussel uses only the Smallmouth and Largemouth Bass as host species. This relationship makes the Wavyrayed Lampmussel completely dependent on healthy populations of the bass. But this remarkable example of co-evolution doesn't end there. To maximize the probability of encountering the right host, the Wavyrayed Lampmussel has devised an elaborate

method of attracting it. The mussel actually goes fishing for the bass, using specialized tissues that extend from the shell and that imitate a minnow. These "lures" vary in type, from a solid bright orange to a complex "minnow" pattern, complete with fins and eye spots. When a hungry bass is drawn in and strikes these tantalizing lures pulsing in the river's current, the female Lampmussel expels thousands of tiny glochidia. The glochidia then attach themselves to the fins and gills of the host fish, thus helping to ensure the next generation of Lampmussels.

Freshwater mussel populations face a broad range of threats. Predators that consume freshwater mussels include Muskrats and Raccoons, as evidenced by the small piles of empty shells, or "middens," that often accumulate at feeding sites along shorelines. In pre-settlement times, mussels were also harvested by First Nations as a food source. While high populations of predators can sometimes contribute to declines of some mussel species, today freshwater mussel populations are primarily threatened by poor water quality, non-sustainable agricultural practices, and urbanization.

Exotic species also pose a significant threat to freshwater

The Wavyrayed Lampmussel attracts its fish host, the Smallmouth Bass, using specialized tissues, or "lures," that imitate food items. The lure pictured here is a bright orange type, but complex "minnow" patterns complete with fins and eye-spots are more common.

The Eastern Sand Darter is a small, translucent member of the perch family that lives on, and burrows in, sand substrates in rivers and large lakes. It is a globally imperilled species that has disappeared from four of seven river systems in the Carolinian region.

mussels within the Carolinian zone. The recent invasion of the Zebra Mussel in Great Lakes waters has devastated populations of native mussels and led to the imperilment of several species. Fortunately, Zebra Mussels have not colonized many of the larger inland rivers of the region, making the Ausable, Grand, and Sydenham rivers important refuges for many species; of the eleven species of freshwater mussels currently listed as endangered and threatened in Canada, all currently live within these river systems.

FISHES

Many people are familiar with the common commercial and sport fishes found in the Carolinian zone. Lake Erie supports a large commercial fishery for Walleye and Yellow Perch, which can be enjoyed fresh in many local restaurants. Angling for Smallmouth Bass is popular throughout the zone, and the Grand River supports a world-renowned Brown Trout fishery. However, there are more than 130 fish species found in the area, most of which are unfamiliar to the angler or casual observer. The Canadian range of about twenty-five of these fishes is entirely or mainly restricted to the Carolinian region.

Fishes in the Carolinian zone inhabit a diverse array of habitats, varying from the open waters of the Great Lakes and large coastal wetlands (for example, Point Pelee and the St. Clair National

Wildlife Area) to the numerous warm-water streams and smaller inland marshes and swamps. With very few natural lakes, the landscape of Carolinian Canada is dominated by warm-water rivers and streams. The greatest diversity of fishes occurs within these flowing waters.

Fishes of the Carolinian zone are as varied as the habitats they occupy. They range in size from the diminutive Least Darter, which is Canada's smallest freshwater fish (with an average length of twenty-five millimetres), to the mighty Lake Sturgeon, which can attain lengths in excess of two metres, weigh more than a hundred kilograms, and live for almost a century. Some Carolinian fishes have very unusual behaviours. The Eastern Sand Darter, for example, spends much of its time either completely buried in the sand or with just its eyes protruding from the substrate — an unusual characteristic among Canadian freshwater fishes. Most Carolinian fish species are small and feed on aquatic insects, worms, and crustaceans. The Golden Redhorse, for example, sucks snails and small clams off the river bottom. There are also several predators at the top of the food chain, such as the Spotted Gar and Muskellunge, which feed voraciously on other fishes.

A broad range of human activities has had a negative impact on fishes in the Carolinian zone. Most of the rivers and streams have dams or other water-control structures that impede migration and alter stream flows. Many wetlands and streams have been drained or channelled to allow or aid agricultural production. Rivers and streams often receive excessive sediment,

Top: The Golden Redhorse is a common inhabitant of most river systems in the Carolinian region. It feeds on insects, worms, and molluscs that it captures off the bottom of waterways.

Above: The Pugnose Shiner is a diminutive member of the minnow family that requires clear, clean water with abundant aquatic plants. Endangered in Canada, it occurs in a few coastal wetlands in the Carolinian region.

The Longear Sunfish is one of Canada's most colourful freshwater fishes. It prefers clear, slow-moving, well-vegetated streams in the Carolinian region.

nutrients, and chemical loads from intensive farming without sufficient buffers. Increased siltation, for example, is thought to be the cause of the disappearance of the Gravel Chub, a streamlined, silvery minnow that used to inhabit fast-water sections of the Thames River, but has not been seen there since 1958.

Urbanization in some parts of the Carolinian zone has altered fish habitat and added pollutants to waterways. Intensive harvest through commercial and sport fishing has also changed fish communities, and the introduction and spread of exotic species has likewise taken its toll. More than 180 exotic aquatic species have been introduced into the Great Lakes Basin, and many of these species, such as the Sea Lamprey, Common Carp, and Round Goby, have had detrimental impacts on populations of native fishes. These exotic species are impossible to eradicate and very difficult and expensive to control.

Twenty-eight species of fishes known (or formerly known) to live in the Carolinian zone have been listed as species at risk, either nationally or provincially, because of ongoing threats, declining populations, and/or limited distributions. One of these, the Blue Pike (also known as the Blue Walleye or Blue Pickerel), is now considered extinct. It formerly occurred in Lake Erie, the Niagara River, and Lake Ontario, but disappeared in the 1960s due to overharvesting, deteriorating habitat conditions, and competition with introduced Rainbow Smelt. The list of Carolinian fishes at risk also includes species such as the Northern Madtom, Eastern Sand Darter, and Pugnose Shiner, which are at risk globally.

However, the news is not all gloom and doom. The Brindled Madtom and Central Stoneroller were recently removed from the list of Canadian and Ontario species at risk, because their populations are secure. Likewise, the status of other fishes at risk, such as the Greenside Darter and the Lake Sturgeon, appears to be improving in the Carolinian zone.

The Brindled Madtom is one of five madtom species that occur in Canada. Madtoms, when handled, can inflict a painful but not dangerous wound through their pectoral fin spines and associated poison glands.

CONSERVATION AND RECOVERY

In the watersheds of southwestern Ontario, Canada's greatest diversity of freshwater fishes and mussels clashes directly with some of the highest levels of human-induced stresses in the country. Not surprisingly, the region has a high proportion of Canada's species at risk, including some of the most imperilled fishes and mussels in North America. For example, the Northern Riffleshell population in the Sydenham River is believed to be one of only four reproducing populations remaining in the world.

A few fishes have already been lost from the region's waterways. With extinction rates for North American freshwater species estimated to be five times higher than those for terrestrial species, immediate and effective conservation action is required to prevent further losses. Fortunately, recent efforts towards freshwater conservation appear to be gaining ground, and many recovery planning efforts for species at risk are already well under way in Carolinian watersheds.

The Sydenham River was the first to attract attention as one of Canada's richest watersheds for aquatic species at risk, and it is recognized as a globally significant freshwater ecosystem. The recovery strategy recently developed for the Sydenham River was the first in the country to adopt an aquatic *ecosystem* approach, as opposed to single-species recovery plans. The ecosystem approach is a logical solution in watersheds where

From its source near the village of Dundalk, just south of Georgian Bay, to its mouth at Port Maitland, on Lake Erie, the Grand River flows three hundred kilometres through the heartland of southern Ontario. There are more than eighty species of fish found in the Grand River watershed, representing 62 percent of all fish species found in Canada, and more than thirty species of mussels.

many of the fish and mussel species at risk occur in the same habitats and share similar threats; recovery actions can be undertaken for the benefit of several species. This multi-species approach is also more cost-effective than the traditional single-species approach. The recently completed Sydenham River Recovery Strategy is now being used as a model for other priority watersheds within the Carolinian zone. These recovery planning initiatives include the Ausable, Grand, and Thames rivers, as well as the Essex-Erie region, which together cover the majority of watersheds within the Carolinian zone. In Carolinian watersheds, the focus of recovery efforts for habitat improvement has been on stewardship activities, such as riparian plantings and fencing of livestock, which help reduce sediment and nutrient loading to watercourses. Other important recovery efforts include research and monitoring of species-at-risk populations, as well as education and increasing public awareness.

Since aquatic species at risk are often the most sensitive indicators of environmental quality, managing ecosystems for their preservation should result in healthy watersheds capable of supporting diverse communities of other native species. These rare and seemingly obscure species of fishes and mussels are the proverbial canaries of the (underwater) coal mine. With the commitment and involvement of concerned citizens to protect and restore the watersheds of greatest priority in Carolinian Canada, we can all help to ensure the preservation of freshwater biodiversity — which bodes well for our own health and quality of life.

CHAPTER 8

Tiny Creatures: Butterflies *and* Other Insects

Paul Pratt

WHEN PEOPLE START PAYING attention to the smaller creatures such as butterflies, it is amazing how many, varied species one can see. More than thirty thousand species of insects have been found in Canada. While no one knows exactly how many different kinds of insects there are in Carolinian Canada, the number is well into the thousands, far more than all the plants and other types of wildlife combined. A single site, such as the Ojibway Prairie Complex in Windsor, may hold more than three thousand insect species.

The largest groups of insects include the flies (Diptera), beetles (Coleoptera), ants and wasps (Hymenoptera), butterflies and moths (Lepidoptera), and bugs (Hemiptera). In just these five groups, it is estimated that approximately twenty thousand species await discovery in Canada. As well, the sheer number of

The Eastern Tiger Swallowtail, appropriately named for its bold, black tiger stripes, is a woodland species, but it can also be found nectaring in fields and along roadsides. Its larvae feed primarily on Tulip-tree and other Carolinian tree species such as Hoptree, along with cherry and ash.

individuals is staggering: leafhoppers may sometimes exceed one million individuals per hectare at some sites. As most of the biological diversity of Carolinian Canada is found in the insect population, and so little of it is known, there are untold treasures for future generations to discover.

BUTTERFLIES

Top: The Common Buckeye, widespread in the U.S., does not overwinter in Ontario; its presence here depends on the annual migration of adult butterflies into the province each year. This territorial butterfly has a rapid flight and is usually seen flying in disturbed areas such as fields and roadsides.

Above: The larvae of Common Buckeye feed on weedy species, such as plantain and toadflax, found in disturbed areas.

Flowering meadows, open woodlands, and sunny breaks in forests support rich assemblages of butterflies in Carolinian Canada. Butterflies of the Carolinian region include Canada's largest butterfly, the Giant Swallowtail, and many species typical of more southern areas, such as the Zebra Swallowtail, Northern Hairstreak, Hackberry Butterfly, Hoary Edge Skipper, Duke's Skipper, and Wild Indigo Duskywing. Butterflies can be found throughout the year in Carolinian Canada. Species such as Mourning Cloak, Eastern Comma, and Milbert's Tortoiseshell hibernate through the winter as adults. During a warm day in winter or early spring, a few butterflies may emerge for a brief appearance long before the first flowers of spring. There are records of Mourning Cloaks for every month of the year. Other butterflies cannot survive winters in Ontario but immigrate into the region each year. In addition to Monarchs, species such as Question Mark, Painted Lady, Red Admiral, and sometimes more southern species such as Fiery Skipper and Common Buckeye invade Ontario in varying numbers each summer.

Natural habitats in Carolinian Canada are highly fragmented, and the butterfly species associated with them are highly susceptible to further habitat loss and fragmentation. For example, the striking Karner Blue was once found in six sites in southern Ontario, but its population was reduced to two locations by the early 1980s: Port Franks and St. Williams. This brilliant blue butterfly depends on a single plant for survival, Wild Lupine, the food plant for the butterfly's caterpillar stage. Lupines in turn depend on fires to maintain their habitat, which is open oak savanna. Without fire, this open habitat becomes a closed canopy forest, and the resulting dense shade will not support lupines — or Karner Blue butterflies. In addition, much of Ontario's remnant savannas were planted with pines before the ecological significance of oak savanna was realized in the 1980s.

Below: Extirpated from Ontario, the Karner Blue butterfly is now the focus of a long-term reintroduction effort at Pinery Provincial Park and nearby sites, where controlled burning is regenerating the butterfly's habitat of oak savanna.

Bottom: The larvae of some butterfly species, such as those of the Eastern Tiger Swallowtail (below), have evolved with fierce-looking markings, which serve to warn off predators. Other adaptations, such as the toxicity of Monarch larvae, also protect butterfly caterpillars from predation by birds.

By 1989, Karner Blue was gone from Ontario. The same fate has befallen other butterfly species dependent on lupines, such as the Frosted Elfin and the Persius Duskywing. There are currently plans being developed to reintroduce the Karner Blue in Ontario, but recovery can be difficult. Karner Blues depend not only on oak savanna habitat with sufficient food plants for their larvae and with nectar sources for the adults; ants are also essential. The caterpillars are "attended" by several ant species, which protect them from predators in return for the sugary "honeydew" produced by the caterpillars. The Edward's Hairstreak Butterfly, another savanna species, also has caterpillars that are closely attended by ants. The caterpillars are kept in the ant nest during the day and carried to their food plants each evening, where they are "milked" for their honeydew. The ants attack any insect trying to approach a caterpillar.

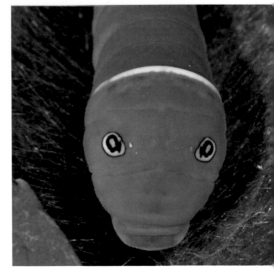

The Eastern Comma is one of the first butterflies to appear in the spring: adults hibernate over the winter and begin to fly on the first warm days of spring. Seen in forest clearings and edges, and along roadsides, it has perfect camouflage: when disturbed it alights on trees, sits upside down, and closes its leaf-shaped wings.

These are just two examples of the complex interactions between insects, interactions that scientists are only beginning to understand.

MOTHS: LEGION OF THE NIGHT

The number of butterfly species is miniscule compared to the huge diversity of moths in Carolinian Canada. They range from giants such as the Cecropia and the Polyphemus, to medium-sized moths such as the Promethea moth and the Tulip-tree Silkmoth, to tiny micro-lepidoptera moths that can live in a single seed or leaf.

The elegant, showy underwing moths are named for the striking contrast between the cryptic bark-like pattern of their forewings and their brightly coloured and boldly patterned hindwings. These large moths belong to the owlet moth family, named for the bright glow of their eyes in a flashlight beam. They have a single brood per year, with the adult moths appearing between mid-July and October. They reach their peak of diversity in oak-hickory woodlots during August. The eggs overwinter before hatching in spring, and the caterpillars feed on various tree species such as walnut, hickories, oaks, and willows. Their quaint common names, such as Darling Underwing, The Sweetheart, and Dejected Underwing reflect the Romantic period of the 1800s, when many underwing moths were first discovered and named.

A good way to observe these moths is to go "sugaring." Mix one cup of sugar, two mashed bananas, one ounce of molasses, and one bottle of beer to make a solution. Sometimes a bit of dry yeast can be added to help with the fermentation process. When this mixture is applied with a paintbrush to tree trunks at dusk, magnificent moths and other insects will visit the trees in the evening to enjoy the sugary concoction. By far the easiest way to observe moths, however, is to pay attention to lights at night. Almost any light will attract a variety of moths, and the light itself aids identification.

SINGING INSECTS

While butterflies appeal to our sense of sight, other insects demand the attention of our ears. The hot days of mid-summer bring on the piercing songs of cicadas during the heat of day and into early evening. Dog-day cicadas remain underground for several years as nymphs before emerging as adults for their brief mating flights. Several cicada species inhabit the Carolinian region, including rare southern species such as the Scissor-grinder Cicada.

Crickets, katydids, and grasshoppers belong to the order Orthoptera, and most have a single generation per year, which

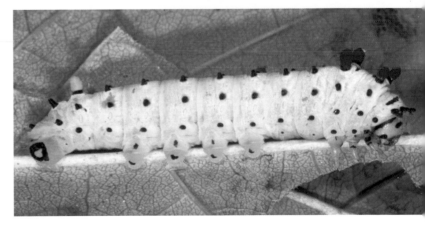

From top to bottom: Although the adult Saddleback moth is plain and inconspicuous, its caterpillar looks quite distinctive, almost like a Scottish Terrier. The caterpillar is capable of inflicting painful stings with its spines, a useful defence against predators. Most moths begin to fly shortly after dusk, but Luna moths are rarely seen because their peak flight period is after midnight. Promethea moth caterpillars feed on Sassafras, a Carolinian tree, and Spicebush, a Carolinian shrub.

Cicadas are distinguished by their large, clear wings, which are held roof-like over their abdomens. Cicadas produce their calls with timbals — paired, drum-like structures on the sides of their abdomens.

matures in late summer. Just as the breeding season is ending for birds, their songs are replaced by much larger numbers of these singing insects. One cannot step outside without hearing the ever-present sound of field crickets, ground crickets, and meadow katydids.

Grasshoppers usually make sound by rubbing their hind legs against their wings or abdomen, or by snapping their wings. Crickets and katydids sing by rubbing their forewings together.

The Northern True Katydid makes one of the characteristic evening sounds of the Carolinian forest from mid-July through August. These large (forty- to fifty-millimetre), near-flightless green insects live high in the crowns of trees. Even dedicated entomologists rarely get to see one. Unlike the trills and buzzy sounds of other katydids, their calls are so loud that they have been mistaken for much larger creatures. Their raucous calling starts at dusk and, on warm evenings, continues well into the night. The onomatopoeic rendition of this song (ka-ty-did) is the source of the common name for this entire group of insects. The endlessly repeated "katydid," "shedid," and "shedidn't" phrases are spaced about one second apart. On warm summer nights, the noise made by large numbers of these remarkable insects can drown out all other forest sounds.

FIREFLIES

All fireflies belong to a family of beetles called the Lampyridae. Approximately 180 species of Lampyridae are found in Canada and the United States. While not all species produce light as adult beetles, all species have luminous larvae. The luminous segments of the abdomen can easily be distinguished by their pale yellow colour.

A firefly's light is turned on or off in response to the air supply to the luminescent organs. Fireflies produce green, yellow, or orange light, depending on the particular species. Some species flash their light for a deadly purpose. Female fireflies of the genus *Photuris* can change their flash pattern to mimic the pattern of the Big Dipper Firefly and other fireflies in

Below: Millions of fireflies have been collected over the past thirty years for scientific and medical research. Firefly luciferin and luciferase are used in cancer research, to detect bacterial contamination in food, and may even be used to test for life on Mars.

Bottom: Singing insects such as the Snowy Tree Cricket, also called the Temperature Cricket, fill the air with loud song. The speed of insects' song is related to temperature, and the most predictable is that of the Temperature Cricket: add the number 40 to the number of pulses in 13 seconds, and that will provide an accurate reading of the temperature in degrees Fahrenheit.

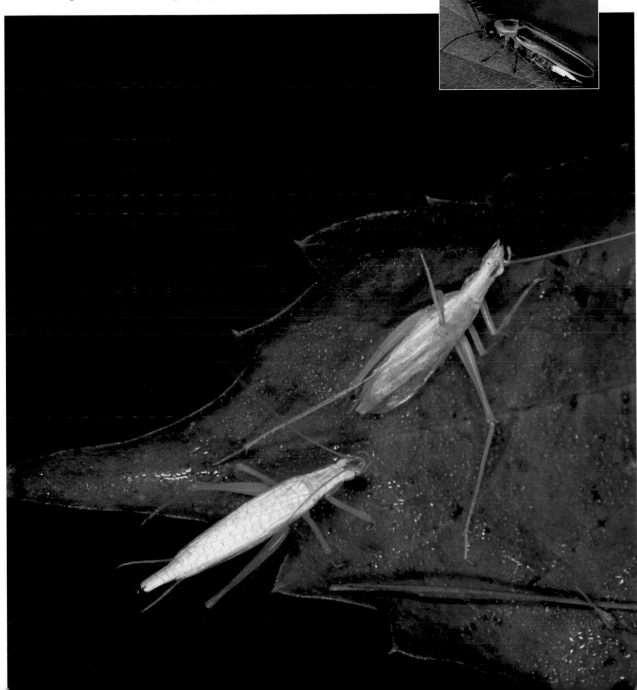

Unlike birds, many insects do not have "official" common names. This insect, *Graphocephala coccinea*, has been called Red-backed Leafhopper, Red-banded Leafhoppper, Candystriped Leafhopper, and Scarlet and Green Leafhopper.

the genus *Photinus*. Female *Photuris* fireflies then capture and eat the males that are attracted to them. This is not just to obtain an extra meal. These males contain defensive chemicals that *Photuris* females lack. When the females ingest them, the chemicals are incorporated into their own bodies and used to repel spiders and other predators.

The Big Dipper Firefly is found across the eastern United States and north to Carolinian Canada. From mid-June through August, it appears over lawns, meadows, and wetland habitats. Big Dipper Fireflies flash a distinctive pattern shortly after sunset, and usually fly less than two metres off the ground. The males rise abruptly into the air during their flashing, producing a yellow "J" stroke. The flash lasts about a half-second. Then the male pauses and flies a short way before repeating its performance. Flashes are produced every five to eight seconds. Females remain perched in the grass and respond after two or three seconds with a half-second flash.

The larvae of different types of fireflies behave in different ways. Some fireflies in the genus *Photinus* are subterranean and likely feed on earthworms. Others, including larvae in the genus *Photuris,* are surface dwellers, feeding on snails and other invertebrates; these are the most commonly seen "glow-worms."

While some species of fireflies have declined in population, the Big Dipper Firefly has probably benefited from the clearing of forests in eastern North America, which creates the grassland or meadow habitat it prefers. It is more widespread now than in historical times.

LEAFHOPPERS AND OTHER SMALL BUGS

The short-horned bugs of the order Homoptera include familiar groups of insects such as cicadas, spittlebugs, planthoppers, treehoppers, and leafhoppers. More than twelve hundred species of leafhopper are found in Canada. Almost any backyard supports several species, including the brilliantly coloured leafhopper *Graphocephala coccinea*.

Leafhoppers (Cicadellidae) and piglet bugs (Caliscelidae) are the most diverse group of insects that specialize in prairie living, with more than two hundred species endemic to North American's prairie habitats. Many species are restricted to high-quality prairie remnants, such as the Ojibway Prairie Complex in Windsor. Other species are restricted to alvars, southern bogs, and Great Lakes shorelines. The dune communities at Ipperwash, on the shores of Lake Huron, support the largest number of imperilled bugs in Canada, some twenty-four species, including

an undescribed *Prairiana* leafhopper known nowhere else in the world.

DRAGONFLIES AND DAMSELFLIES

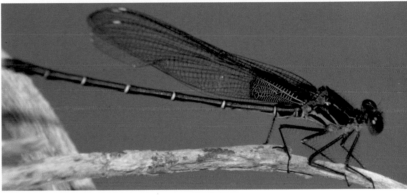

Dragonflies and damselflies of the order Odonata are second only to butterflies in their popular appeal. Anyone who has had a dragonfly whiz by and catch a biting deer fly can appreciate these swift insect predators. The Carolinian region supports a large number of dragonfly and damselfly species found nowhere else in Canada, and in recent years new species have been discovered almost annually. However, this region also has the greatest threats to dragonfly populations due to the highly altered landscape. Some species have already disappeared.

Canada's largest dragonfly, the Swamp Darner, breeds in woodland ponds of the Carolinian region. In places such as Skunk's Misery, northeast of Chatham, it can be seen hawking for insects in forest clearings and wooded lanes. The large, blue-eyed Spadderdock Darner is found only at Fish Point on Pelee Island, where it is abundant. As well, the rivers and streams of southwestern Ontario provide habitat for species not found elsewhere in Canada. For example, damselflies such as American Rubyspot, Smoky Rubyspot, Blue-ringed Dancer, and Dusky Dancer are found along the Sydenham and Thames rivers.

Top: Bluets are a genus of narrow-winged damselflies. The adult males are typically coloured blue and black. Most species prefer ponds and marshy habitats, but a few are found along streams.

Above: The bright ruby base of the forewings of the American Rubyspot make this large damselfly easy to identify. It is found along the larger rivers of southwestern Ontario.

The Twelve-spotted Skimmer is one of the most common and widespread dragonflies of southern Ontario.

The north shore of Lake Erie hosts a spectacular staging of migratory insects, particularly dragonflies, each September. In addition to the Monarch butterflies, huge numbers of Common Green Darner and Black Saddlebag dragonflies can be seen swarming around the tip of Point Pelee National Park. Southern species such as Spot-winged Glider, Carolina Saddlebags, and Red Saddlebags can usually be found in the mix at this time of year. The Monarchs are on their long flight to central Mexico for the winter but, amazingly, no one knows where the dragonflies are heading. Research is under way to unravel this mystery.

IT IS COMMON TO hear of a new insect species for Canada or even a new species to science being discovered in the Carolinian region. However, many of these are restricted to small patches of continually shrinking habitat such as oak savanna. Other species have already disappeared and many more are threatened.

Habitat loss continues to be the leading threat to insect populations in the region. Habitats maintained by fire, such as prairies and oak savanna, require active management, with

prescribed burning. Fortunately, fire is becoming a more prevalent management tool in southern Ontario, and many prairie and savanna sites, such as Pinery, Rondeau, Turkey Point, and Ojibway Prairie Complex, are now being burned on a regular basis. Hundreds of insect species will benefit from the protection, stewardship, and restoration of oak savanna and other important habitats in the Carolinian region. Considering insects' complexity and the essential role they play in food webs and as pollinators, it is imperative to incorporate insects into the recovery strategies and management of our remaining native habitat remnants.

Along with the beauty and complexity of the insect world, there is still much mystery. Volunteers play a key role in adding to our understanding of insects, particularly butterflies. For example,

The Monarch is one of our most readily recognizable butterflies, commonly seen in meadows and fields where the caterpillar's food plant, milkweed, and abundant nectar-filled flowers for adults are found. In autumn, Monarchs congregate by the thousands along the shores of Lake Erie and Lake Ontario in preparation for their annual migration to wintering grounds in Mexico.

one-day butterfly counts sponsored by the North American Butterfly Association and held each year across Canada and the United States provide crucial information about the health of butterfly populations. Such monitoring activities are held in Carolinian Canada between late June and mid-August at insect "hotspots," such as Pinery, Skunk's Misery, Clear Creek Forest, Long Point, Ojibway Prairie Complex, Point Pelee, and Pelee Island. Counts from Carolinian Canada often record more than fifty species, and include the highest totals for all of Canada.

Very few of Carolinian Canada's rare insects have been designated as endangered or threatened, and even fewer are protected by law. There is still too little known about insects to accurately determine the status of the vast majority of species. Much needs to be done — by professional entomologists, dedicated amateurs, and volunteers alike — to increase our understanding of these amazing animals.

Top: Although rare in Ontario, American Snout can easily be seen at Point Pelee in August. The caterpillar feeds on Hackberry, a common tree at Pelee.

Above: Multicoloured Asian Lady Beetles and Seven-spotted Lady Beetles are now the most commonly seen lady beetles in Ontario. They were introduced to North America because they were seen as beneficial insects: both the adults and the larvae feed on aphids.

PART III

CARING FOR NATURE
ON THE EDGE

INTRODUCTION *to* PART III

Tom Beechey

CAROLINIAN CANADA IS A ZONE of outstanding ecological variety and home to one of the highest concentrations of species at risk in the country. Representing a unique ecological crossroads in North America, its splendour and its vulnerability make it a top priority for nature conservation in Canada.

Surprisingly, dedicated efforts to conserve Carolinian species and spaces are relatively recent, even though some of Canada's first protected areas, such as Queen Victoria Niagara Falls Park, established in 1887, and Rondeau Provincial Park, in 1894, represent early flagships for the cause. And although many other parks and conservation areas were established during the twentieth century, together they account for only approximately 2 percent of the region. In recent decades, environmental designations and a push to encourage private stewardship have built on early efforts and helped to shape the rudiments of a conservation strategy for the zone.

The initial focus of the Carolinian Canada Program reflected the "collector's approach" of the day. The effort originally focused on acquiring thirty-eight natural areas, identified to protect ecosystems and species not yet or only poorly represented in formally protected areas across the region. As work proceeded to secure these areas, efforts were also made to contact and to work with landowners within the zone, in order to provide information and to encourage the owners to protect the Carolinian communities and species on their land. This important phase was later aided by incentives such as property tax rebates. In the 1990s, new views on biodiversity conservation and on the design of protected areas emerged, prompting the Carolinian Canada Coalition to develop a more comprehensive outlook and to revamp the initial conservation strategy. The result was an

Through the commitment of landowners, governments, public agencies, and non-profit organizations, natural areas in Carolinian Canada are being protected. Along with direct purchase of priority land, creative conservation tools include tax incentives and conservation easements.

ecological vision called "The Big Picture," which recognizes the need for a comprehensive network of natural "core" areas and "corridors" connecting them.

Solid ecological assessments are essential tools in the fight to conserve Carolinian species and ecosystems. The development of the Natural Heritage Information Centre (NHIC) in the early 1990s provided conservationists with additional expertise and the capacity to compile, map, and analyze the by now extensive scientific documentation on the region. These new capabilities let scientists model "Big Picture" conservation scenarios and aid the Coalition in planning projects and setting priorities for its work, especially important in light of the limited resources available to help the species and areas most in need of conservation. Once the species and areas are protected, the NHIC's automated databanks, along with field surveys, facilitate long-term monitoring of species and communities, to assess the effectiveness of conservation efforts and to enable practitioners to respond to an ever-changing situation.

Three creeks — Spring, Sulphur, and Ancaster — flow through the Dundas Valley. Carved by an ancient river, the Erigan, as it emptied into glacial Lake Iroquois, the wooded valley is wedged between two escarpment cliffs, where scenic waterfalls cascade over rocks.

While considerable progress has been made on protecting Carolinian biodiversity, there is still much to do. Ongoing work includes conducting ecological surveys, securing natural areas, conserving linkages and corridors, protecting aquatic ecosystems, restoring degraded sites, re-introducing native species, and controlling invasive species. The members of the Carolinian Canada Coalition continue to promote and support private stewardship, educate people about the zone, research, monitor, report on and celebrate progress, and, above all, find money and inspire people to make it all happen. The good news is that spirited collaboration and independent efforts under an inclusive Carolinian Canada banner are having an effect. Together we have taken great strides towards securing a fragile heritage, and with energy and renewed commitment we can surmount the challenges ahead.

CHAPTER 9

HUMAN FOOTPRINTS *in* CAROLINIAN CANADA

Michael Troughton and William DeYoung

From the time that First Nations first hunted in the region, through early European settlement, to the present, Carolinian Canada has a long history of human dependence on the lands and waters of the region.

HUMAN HISTORY IN THE Carolinian zone goes back to the end of the last Ice Age, between eleven thousand and thirteen thousand years ago, when the first Paleo-Indian hunters arrived soon after the glacial ice retreated. The Paleo-Indians may have witnessed and perhaps contributed to the extinction of mastodons and mammoths that roamed the area. As the climate and vegetation altered, these nomadic hunters migrated north, following their key food source, the caribou. For the next eight thousand years, the Carolinian region became home to a sequence of Indian populations, during what archaeologists have named the successive Archaic and Woodland periods. The Indian inhabitants occupied a varied landscape of thick forest and more open savanna areas. The forest was well stocked with food, including game, especially deer and beaver, many nuts and berries, and flocks of migrating birds. In addition, there were abundant quantities of fish in rivers flowing into Lakes St. Clair, Erie, and Ontario.

As early as eight thousand years ago, cultural innovations leading to agriculture took place in Central America, specifically the domestication of corn (maize), beans, and several vegetables, including squashes. Cultivation eventually spread into humid southeastern North America, and was adopted by Indian groups occupying the Eastern Hardwood Forests. Cultivation supported larger numbers of people, a more sedentary life, and more sophisticated cultures. Nevertheless, cultivation was semi-shifting in nature, and was carried out on small fields, which were periodically cleared close to village sites and then abandoned after a few years to revert to forest vegetation.

Agriculture based on shifting cultivation spread into the Great Lakes Basin, where evidence suggests that corn was introduced into southern Ontario by 500 AD, in the Late Woodland Period. Farming supported local population increases and more permanent settlements of multi-family longhouses in fortified villages, in the midst of their cultivated garden plots. However, diets continued to include meat from game, fruits and nuts, and fish from the rivers and lakes of the rich Carolinian forest zone. (A re-created Iroquoian village, Ska-Nah-Doht, can be visited at the Longwoods Conservation Area southwest of London.)

By 1600 AD, Iroquoian agriculturalists, known as the Neutrals (or Attawandaron), occupied much of the Carolinian region. During the early seventeenth century, French Recollet and Jesuit missionaries and fur traders visited the area. While the priests' records have supplied valuable information on the contemporary native culture, the priests were also part of the European influence that helped destroy much of the Indian occupancy in the Carolinian zone. European diseases, especially smallpox, killed many Indians. They also lost their lives through warfare fought between the new colonial powers of France and Britain and their Indian allies to control territory and the fur trade.

In 1651-52 the Neutrals were defeated and dispersed by Mohawk and Seneca Iroquois from south of Lake Ontario. For the next century, Indian occupancy of the Carolinian region was heavily reduced, although some Chippewa moved in and replaced the Neutrals, whose survivors were absorbed by Iroquois to the south. Population reduction and dispersal from the area meant that, from the 1650s to the 1760s, the forest vegetation recovered much of its pre-agricultural character and remained relatively undisturbed until settlement began in the late eighteenth century.

EUROPEAN OCCUPANCY OF CAROLINIAN CANADA

Prior to 1760, the Carolinian region was part of the eastern forest interior that was controlled by France, but was largely set aside as a zone for fur trading with its Indian inhabitants rather than being viewed as open for settlement or cultivation as farmland. The only permanent settlements were scattered forts and trading posts (for example, Detroit), from which French-Canadian fur traders travelled inland, including into the Thames (*La Tranchee*) and Grand watersheds. The situation changed, however, after the 1760 British takeover of Quebec, and especially after the 1776 American War of Independence, which transformed southwestern Ontario into a frontier buffer zone between the two Anglo-Saxon powers on the continent. The British built additional forts at Malden (Amherstburg), Newark (Niagara-on the Lake), and York (Toronto), and the 1780s saw initial attempts at European settlement in the southwest, the beginnings of British attempts to establish a farm-based agrarian economy. For the Carolinian region, this was the beginning of widespread forest removal.

Early settlers were both impressed and intimidated by the extent and density of the forest, which was hard to traverse and difficult to clear. Records from the period suggest that many settlers perceived the forest as "the enemy," which may account for the vehemence with which they pursued felling and burning. Undoubtedly, the thick forest posed problems insofar as the new Colonial government's objective was to survey the land into townships, within which a concession-and-lot grid was to be the basis for individual landholding and the establishment of farms. It was a daunting task to establish access roads and to locate lot parcels in what was still a "wilderness." However, settlement schemes such as that of the Talbot Settlement along the Lake Erie shore, and government roads such as Dundas Street, facilitated access.

A series of treaties was signed between 1764 and 1827, which transferred the majority of the Carolinian-zone lands from Indians to the British, the exceptions being reserves, the majority of which were later further reduced. For European settlers, a 1791 Settlement Duty

Fishing with bamboo poles, the Hess and O'Brian families catch pike in the Old Ausable River at the Pinery, in 1909.

While much of the extensive marshland that once existed in Carolinian Canada was drained to make way for agriculture and settlement, some large areas, such as the Lake St. Clair Marshes, remain. This marsh complex is a major stopping point for migratory birds. Tens of thousands of Tundra Swans, ducks, geese, and other birds congregate here in the spring and autumn.

regulation stipulated that a settler had to clear and fence five acres, clear half the road allowance, and build a house of sixteen by twenty feet. Land clearance was for fields in which to grow wheat and other crops such as peas and potatoes. The forest offered grazing for livestock and other items for domestic subsistence. The small population and primitive tools meant that, for the first forty years of settlement, the 1780s to the 1820s, clearance was limited; it was hard for a farm family to clear more than a few acres per year.

The Carolinian region was a major theatre in the War of 1812–14. Battles were fought in the southwest (Battle of the Thames near Moraviantown) and the Niagara peninsula (Queenston Heights, Lundy's Lane). Forts and towns (including Malden, Newark, and York) were burnt, and most farms, taverns, and mills were destroyed. However, when the war ended, and especially after the end of the Napoleonic conflict in Europe in 1815, settlers, including disbanded troops, Americans, and those affected by the post-war depression in Britain, began to arrive, and clearance accelerated. While some marshes and bogs were avoided as too wet and some river and stream-valley sides as too steep, the majority of Carolinian lands were found to be fertile and suitable for cultivation, and felling and burning gathered pace.

Land clearance expanded greatly across the Carolinian counties (here meaning those counties located entirely within or with large parts within the Carolinian zone) after 1830, as settlers flowed into the region. By 1880, 88 percent of Carolinian Canada was settled, and only 40 percent of farmland was woodlot. By 1911, woodlot remained on only 12.2 percent of farmed property. Thus, a pattern of forest clearance was firmly established by the beginning of the twentieth century.

Sawmills in Carolinian Canada, such as this one in Goderich, still active in 1906, contributed significantly to the regional economy, providing timber for manufacturing.

THE AGE OF WOOD

The nineteenth century has been called "the Age of Wood." Wood was certainly the primary material for building and manufacturing throughout the Carolinian zone. From the 1830s to the 1850s, the Carolinian region was a primary timber zone in Upper Canada, and its timber resources were rapidly exploited. Hundreds of sawmills processed wood for local use and export. In the 1850s, the pine stands of Norfolk supported the largest sawmilling employment in the province. Potash made from wood ashes was used in soap manufacture, and the bark of oak and Eastern Hemlock was crushed and processed to make tannin. Timber and sawn lumber became Canada's main export.

The combined impact of widespread demand for wood and the acceleration of clearance for farming meant that, by the time of Confederation in 1867, a majority of the Carolinian forest was cleared, and the rural area had developed into the most

As land was cleared for farming in the nineteenth century, a typical pattern evolved: clearance was from the front to the back of lots, such that farm woodlots were left as linear features running parallel between concession roads — a pattern that can still be distinguished today in Carolinian Canada's farmland.

productive agrarian economy in Canada. Thousands of individual farms, plus hundreds of small settlements, the majority of which were farm-service villages and small towns, had transformed the original forest into a largely cleared and cultivated landscape. Most farms had moved from production to simply meet domestic needs to a commercial farm economy. Wheat remained the chief crop and export item until mid-century, but thereafter there was a growing emphasis on livestock, notably dairy cattle for milk and cheese production, except in the extreme southwest, where cash-cropping continued to dominate.

Carolinian counties still accounted for substantial amounts of timber and firewood production in the late 1800s. The 1880–81 Census records more than seventeen hundred establishments and eight thousand workers directly involved in wood-processing and manufacturing in the Carolinian counties. While most pine had been harvested, the Carolinian zone yielded more than four million cubic feet of oak (77 percent of the provincial total), together with significant amounts of elm, maple, walnut, and hickory. Large quantities came from the extreme southwest, where drainage of the extensive remaining wetlands was taking place. The Carolinian region also yielded more than 35 percent of the total cords of firewood in the province, important at a time when wood was the primary fuel.

At the price of its own massive depletion, the forest had played a significant role in the success of the agrarian society. As late as 1914, the remaining forest still contributed to a regional timber industry, and local wood-based manufacturing was typical of all villages, towns, and cities, while farmers used their woodlots for building materials for barns and fences, as well as for fuel and some maple-syrup production — uses that continue to this day.

THE URBAN AND INDUSTRIAL ECONOMY

By the second half of the nineteenth century, the Carolinian zone was emerging as one of the key areas of urban and industrial growth in Canada. The railway era, beginning in the 1850s, began the transformation and supported the concentration of manufacturing in Toronto, Hamilton, London, and other cities along the urban-transportation "corridor." Part of the remaining forest was consumed over the next forty years to fuel the

locomotives and steam engines used in industrial manufacturing. Urbanization and industrialization caused further losses of both farm and forest land, especially after the Second World War, as rapid residential and industrial expansion took place around all the region's cities and towns, but especially in the "Golden Horseshoe," from Toronto to Niagara.

The rural-agricultural landscape has also experienced radical changes, especially in the last fifty to sixty years. By 1941, the number of farms had declined to 55,500, although the farmed areas as a percentage of all land in the Carolinian counties remained high at 85 percent, but only 8.5 percent of farmland was in woodland. However, by 1971, farm numbers had fallen to thirty-five thousand (virtually the same as in 1850), farmland had fallen to 76 percent total area, and farm woodland to 7.5 percent of farmland. The latest figures indicate a further huge drop in farm numbers, but still occupying roughly the same total land

The Grand River and its tributaries have been designated a Canadian Heritage River System in recognition of the watershed's rich cultural and natural history.

Ginseng, mainly exported to Asia for medicinal purposes, is a crop commonly grown in the sandy soils of Norfolk County, replacing the once ubiquitous tobacco fields. The shade covers mimic the light conditions found in ginseng's natural habitat, the forest floor.

area. However, an encouraging trend is that, according to the 1996 Census, 12.2 percent of farmland is woodland.

There has been an overall intensification of production, as well as an important division between farming that has "industrialized" through large-scale mechanization and specialization and that which remains less capital-intensive, including both part-time and hobby farms. The Carolinian zone has seen the rise and decline of tobacco, and the emergence of corn and soybeans as field crops, at the expense of hay and oats. Among the industrial farms, specialization in corn and soybeans as cash and feed crops supports intensive cattle, pig, and poultry production. This places pressure on the remaining natural vegetation in the zone, by field enlargement and by reduced grazing, as most animals are housed. Much of the land freed from grazing is now intensively cropped. The result has been widespread removal of woodlots, hedgerows, and permanent pasture.

Interestingly, one crop that is becoming more common in the region is the native Carolinian forest plant American Ginseng, which is being grown on farms for the herbal-remedy market. Natural ginseng populations were overharvested from forests in the zone to the point that this species is now listed as endangered, but the plant is widely cultivated as a partial replacement crop for tobacco, which until recently was farmed extensively in the zone's sandy soils. As well, the Carolinian zone, in particular the Niagara region, is currently the location of the majority of Ontario's vineyards and expanding wine production.

The steep slopes and thin limestone soils of the Niagara Escarpment, which traverses the Carolinian region from the Niagara frontier to Milton, have proven unsuitable for agriculture and remain forested in many areas. The valleys of major rivers and streams, such as the Grand, Thames, and Credit, have also posed problems for cultivation. Likewise, some flood plains have ensured retention of significant woodland, including those in urban tracts. Several First Nation Reserves and territories abut major river valleys, notably the Six Nations on the Grand, the Moraviantown, Chippewa, Munsee-Delaware and Oneida on the Thames, and Walpole Island on the St. Clair, and each contains above-average amounts of natural cover.

SHIFTING PERCEPTIONS

Many Canadian writers, in historical accounts, diaries, and literature, have depicted the early settlers' perception of the bush as a formidable and even frightening force in their lives. Kenneth Kelly has written about the hostility of early-nineteenth-century settlers in Ontario towards the forest, caused partly by the barrier it posed to clearance, together with fear of its predators. He also shows how the farmers' attitudes towards the forest changed throughout the century. This antagonism, Kelly believes, accounted for the massive removal of trees across southern Ontario — more than 60 percent of the forest by 1860. In the next decades, improvements in drainage, attendant on the *Ontario Farm Tile Drainage Act* of 1878, speeded further clearance of wetland sites. By 1900 there were shortages of building timber and fuel and, in addition, problems of rapid runoff and soil erosion due to lack of forest cover. Gradually, this led to a realization of the ecological value of forests and calls for retention and, if possible, enlargement. Despite efforts at conservation that began between the world wars and led to the *Conservation Authorities Act* (1946) and the placing of virtually all the Carolinian zone within individual Conservation Authorities, the overall increases have been relatively small, and have often been offset by pressures from industrial agriculture to enlarge farm fields and by rapid urban,

The moderate climate of the Carolinian region supports Ontario's world-famous wine industry.

suburban, and ex-urban expansion. Unfortunately, losses to urban expansion have offset expansion and retention of woodland on part-time hobby farms and estate lots. On the other hand, one development that has helped to preserve the natural Carolinian vegetation, including both forest and tallgrass prairie, has been the establishment of Conservation Areas within each of the Conservation Authorities. The Conservation Areas, together with major parks such as Rondeau, Long Point, Point Pelee, The Pinery, and Komoka, are the main foci of outdoor recreation in the Carolinian zone.

During each period, humans have regarded the Carolinian landscape from a different perspective, and understanding these perspectives is essential to understanding the values placed upon the landscape throughout history. One could say that, over time and with respect to the natural history of the Carolinian region, its human occupants have shifted their approach from one of functioning *within* a natural ecosystem, to one of working *outside and against* nature, to the present situation — awareness of the need to work *with* nature again. Future approaches and where they eventually take us will depend on the values — ecological, economic, and cultural — we place on the land as we continue to shape the Carolinian landscape.

CHAPTER 10

STEWARDSHIP *in* ACTION

Ric Symmes

THE NATURALIST NETWORK WAS buzzing. The West Elgin Nature Club had discovered Big Bluestem, Compass Plant, Blazing-star, and Gray-headed Coneflower, all tallgrass prairie species, in the midst of Ontario's most active farmland. These plants were thriving along an abandoned rail line not far from Dutton, where railway ownership had prevented cultivation and preserved the native sod and seedbank.

Some adjoining farmers saw this patch of abandoned land as a "weedy" expanse, ripe for cultivation. But Bill Prieksaitis, a broad-shouldered farmer himself, and president of the West Elgin Nature Club, saw a different opportunity. He realized that

Restoration activities such as controlled burns have helped maintain the ecological health of a prairie remnant along an abandoned rail line near Dutton. Prime habitat for butterflies, the Dutton Prairie is also home to a rare population of Compass Plant.

Among the native plants flourishing in the Dutton Prairie are typical tallgrass prairie species such as Indian Grass, Big Bluestem, and Gray-headed Coneflower. It is likely that small fires, ignited by sparks from trains, maintained this prairie remnant over the years.

this remnant was a Carolinian treasure and presented a chance to save a small but significant example of prairie in Ontario. It would not be right, he reasoned, to let this slip away.

To many, this seemed a hopeless dream. The rail line had changed hands, the owner was far away, the land area was small, and the West Elgin Nature Club was not wealthy enough to buy the property, even if the owner could be found and was willing to sell. Nevertheless, Bill Prieksaitis started making inquiries. He traced the ownership to CSX, a company in the United States, and there, by some magic, he found a responsive decision-maker. An engaging and persuasive man of strong conviction, Bill negotiated an agreement to lease two miles of abandoned rail line, about twenty-four acres of land. The West Elgin Nature Club proudly supported the plan and accepted the lease in 1999, with the support of the West Elgin Stewardship Council. Thus, an important piece of Ontario's natural heritage was secured through the creativity and determination of a few dedicated individuals. And their work continues. The group has managed the land to enhance the tallgrass prairie — removing invasive species, conducting controlled burns, and nurturing this rare remnant.

The success of the Dutton Prairie is just one example of the diverse stewardship efforts of many individuals and groups who are working to save what remains of Carolinian Canada's natural areas.

THE EVOLUTION OF CONSERVATION ACTION

Conservation activity in the Carolinian region — and, indeed, in Ontario generally — has evolved over the years. Leadership, methods, and resources have matured from the early efforts of some isolated individuals, through the post–Second World War rise of government agencies, to a return of citizen action in the 1970s, government cutbacks in the 1990s, and most recently to new players, new tools, and a more inclusive approach.

In the early part of the twentieth century, southwestern Ontario was emerging from the pioneer phase, in which nature was seen as boundless and sometimes threatening. Conservation efforts were few and depended on private initiatives by individuals, such as Jack Miner, who campaigned to restore the depleted Canada Goose population, using his nature reserve near

Kingsville, Ontario. The few provincial parks that existed at the time were oriented to recreation, not to the protection of natural heritage. The importance of preserving viable biological communities had little currency; government agencies were small, and conservation was not a public-policy issue.

A series of "natural" disasters sparked a growing awareness that something was wrong with the way land and nature were "managed" in the province. Decades of deforestation, in particular on land with light, sandy soils, turned areas of southern Ontario into virtual deserts in the early years of the twentieth century. Photographs from this period show farms in some Carolinian counties, such as Norfolk, that resemble sandy deserts of the southwestern United States. In times of heavy rain or spring thaw, the loss of forest cover and marshes left the river valleys with little capacity to regulate or absorb runoff, resulting in unmoderated swings from flood to drought conditions. These flood events reached

The Fanshawe Dam, on the north branch of the Thames River in London, is one of the many dams built in the Carolinian region to regulate water flows and prevent flooding.

With the 1961 acquisition of Spooky Hollow Sanctuary, near Turkey Point, the Hamilton Naturalists' Club became the first volunteer organization in Ontario to purchase a significant area as a nature sanctuary. The sixty-seven-hectare site includes a number of different Carolinian forest habitats, from hemlock forest to pine plantation, and the club is engaged in ongoing efforts to re-establish the original oak savanna.

a disastrous peak with the devastating Hurricane Hazel, which struck southern Ontario in 1954. Eighty-one people died and four thousand were left homeless.

In 1946, in response to the flooding events and dustbowl conditions of the 1930s, the provincial government had created a network of Conservation Authorities, whose mandate was to protect "hazard" lands, steep slopes, and lands subject to flooding. Resource management and protection of people and property was their mandate and priority, but protection of nature was a fortunate side benefit.

The early efforts of Conservation Authorities and other government agencies were focused on soil loss, flooding, and reforestation, but didn't address other root causes, like the loss of wetlands. This response was understandable when recovering from disaster. But in some cases, this approach created a new set of problems. For example, in an effort to stop the dust storms and loss of topsoil experienced in the "dirty thirties," governments created plantations such as those at Port Franks, where pine was planted on native oak savanna. As a result, a diverse habitat was replaced by a monoculture of pine trees, leading to the loss of savanna-dependent species such as the Karner Blue butterfly. Similarly, measures to address flooding often involved building dams and other structures, with unintended consequences. Dams flooded wetlands and sometimes blocked the free movement of fish and other wildlife to the headwaters.

Despite the problems, these early efforts by Conservation Authorities to secure flood-plain lands in river valleys preserved some of the finest remaining habitats in the Carolinian region. Other important results included plans and a new watershed management policy that supported agencies buying land to protect soils and water in the public interest. Biological conservation became an important achievement by Conservation Authorities in the Carolinian region.

CONSERVATION IN THE CAROLINIAN REGION

Organizations such as Ontario Nature (formerly the Federation of Ontario Naturalists), the Hamilton Naturalists' Club, and the Nature Conservancy of Canada have been acquiring and protecting land in Carolinian Canada for decades. The protection of significant Carolinian sites, such as Stone Road Alvar, Middle Island, Spooky Hollow Sanctuary, and Short Hills Nature Sanctuary, is due to their

efforts. As well, organizations such as the Lower Grand River Land Trust and Norfolk Land Trust have been acquiring Carolinian properties in order to protect them in perpetuity. This work, along with continued stewardship and ecological restoration of these properties by volunteers, has been crucial. However, it was not until the 1980s that conservation efforts specifically devoted to the region began to take shape. The most important development was the creation of the Carolinian Canada Program in 1984, one of the first projects of the newly formed Natural Heritage League (NHL) initiated by "Terk" Bayly, Monte Hummel, and Bill Sargeant. The Natural Heritage League was a coalition of government agencies, which included the Ministry of Natural Resources, Conservation Authorities, and the

Landowners, Conservation Authorities, and provincial park naturalists are helping the rare songbird Prothonotary Warbler by installing nesting boxes in suitable habitat such as buttonbush swamps. The nest boxes are designed to exclude cowbirds and species such as the House Wren and Tree Swallow that compete for tree cavities.

Stone Road Alvar, on Pelee Island, is one of thirty-eight Carolinian Canada Signature Sites designated as high conservation priorities in the region. Through the committed effort of many individuals, organizations, and governments, many of these sites are now protected.

Ontario Heritage Foundation, working with non-governmental organizations such as the World Wildlife Fund, Ontario Nature, and the Nature Conservancy of Canada. This partnership worked to secure and protect at least one example of all habitat types in southwestern Ontario. Under this scheme, biologists identified thirty-eight critical sites — unprotected natural areas in the zone — as being top priorities for protection. A fundraising effort, spearheaded by the Natural Heritage League, raised money to conserve portions of these sites. At the same time, NHL began a massive effort to contact the private landowners who owned a significant portion of these thirty-eight critical sites. The influential book *Islands of Green*, by Stewart Hilts, Malcolm Kirk, and Ron Reid, describes how the natural values on these important sites might be saved. This landowner-contact program was a unique approach to conservation at the time.

Recognizing that landowners played a key role in the protection of natural areas, the landowner-contact program, led by individuals such as Stewart Hilts at the University of Guelph, appealed to farmers and other rural landowners through personal visits, literally knocking on doors and talking to landowners about stewardship and the unique features of the landscape in an effort to build understanding, conservation support, and a sense of pride. This approach proved very successful, and these critical sites remain largely intact today as a result of securement and efforts to engage the support of private landowners. While the approach was pioneered in the Carolinian region, it has since been used in other areas of Canada, such as British Columbia, to engage private landowners in the important work of land protection.

Much of the conservation activities carried out in the 1980s was stimulated by funding from the Ontario Heritage Foundation, the Ministry of Natural Resources, Wildlife Habitat Canada, and the Ivey Foundation. This changed abruptly in the 1990s, with the economic recession and widespread government cutbacks. "Smaller government" meant that government support funds dried up, and the Ministry of Natural Resources was forced to withdraw much of its presence in the Carolinian zone. Conservation Authorities lost all of their direct provincial funding, and some, driven by local municipal leadership, considered commercial logging of conservation lands. This radical turn of events had a profound and lasting effect on public attitudes. Gone was any illusion that government alone would look after nature and the environment. To

Native plant nurseries such as Pterophylla are key players in the restoration movement, growing native species for use in naturalization projects. By propagating seed from local genetic stock, they are helping to preserve the biodiversity of Carolinian Canada's unique species.

Volunteer stewards Peter Carson and Mary Gartshore, with the assistance of the Norfolk Field Naturalists and other groups, are restoring a twenty-hectare property owned by Ken Stead to oak savanna. In 1995, prior to planting, the ground was prepared for extensive seeding with savanna species sourced from the local area.

protect nature, communities and individuals had to get involved, find new tools, and take action.

In response to the cutback crisis, individuals and small groups in the Carolinian region took up the challenge, using a broad range of approaches at the regional and local level. Two individuals who have worked to protect and restore nature in the region are Mary Gartshore and Peter Carson, whose efforts provide an inspirational example of everything that individuals can accomplish.

Mary and Peter bought a disused tobacco farm near Walsingham, just north of Long Point, and in the 1990s began the work of restoring the sandy fields to tallgrass prairie habitat. Experimenting with a number of different restoration techniques and documenting the results, so that their experiences could be useful to others, they have treated their project as a "laboratory" of sorts — organizing work weekends with naturalist groups, sharing their knowledge, spreading the word. At the same time, they started a native plant nursery, Pterophylla, at the farm, collecting and propagating seeds from local natural areas and making plants available to other restoration projects and to gardeners interested in growing native plants in their yards. Where tobacco once grew, there are now flourishing fields of tallgrass prairie plants. Species of insects never before recorded in the region have found this refuge, and the numbers of bird species visiting or breeding here expands every year. As well, Mary and Peter have been instrumental in facilitating the protection of adjacent lands in the South Walsingham forest complex, working with conservation-minded landowners and

undertaking an outstanding example of oak savanna restoration on old tobacco lands. Their efforts also led the Nature Conservancy of Canada to acquire other land in the vicinity.

Mary and Peter's work has made a significant difference to the acres they steward, but more than that, their efforts have inspired similar projects throughout the Carolinian region, showing all that can be done through commitment, passion, and hard work.

BIG PICTURE CORES AND CORRIDORS

At the same time as protection and restoration work by individuals and local groups was expanding rapidly, conservation science also advanced, informing the work of both the public and practitioners. Scientists determined that saving fragments and the best natural remnants through parks and other types of protected areas is necessary — but not sufficient. The 1980s approach of preserving "islands of green" had significant limitations in terms of effectiveness. A small or isolated pool of habitat is often more vulnerable to disturbance, and local species are more likely to be lost. However, large or connected natural areas are more resilient, generally having greater genetic diversity and proving better able to withstand stresses such as disease and excessive predation.

Led by Reed Noss and other scientists, the emphasis has shifted to creating connections, or "networks of green" — literally, natural corridors — between core areas, which are areas of sufficient size to support healthy populations of diverse species and to better protect

In just over a decade, the Stead property is returning to a diverse ecosystem, and is now used for research and education.

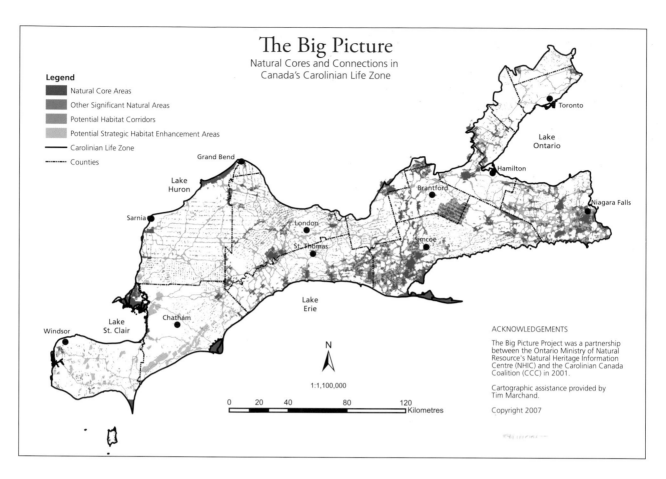

The Big Picture
Natural Cores and Connections in Canada's Carolinian Life Zone

Legend
- ■ Natural Core Areas
- ■ Other Significant Natural Areas
- ■ Potential Habitat Corridors
- ■ Potential Strategic Habitat Enhancement Areas
- —— Carolinian Life Zone
- ‑‑‑‑ Counties

ACKNOWLEDGEMENTS

The Big Picture Project was a partnership between the Ontario Ministry of Natural Resource's Natural Heritage Information Centre (NHIC) and the Carolinian Canada Coalition (CCC) in 2001.

Cartographic assistance provided by Tim Marchand.

Copyright 2007

1:1,100,000

The "Big Picture" map, sponsored by the Carolinian Canada Coalition and prepared using advanced GIS technology, paints a picture of how existing natural areas could be linked together to create a natural heritage network of habitats. This network of core areas and green corridors is crucial to maintain biodiversity in a productive, human-dominated landscape.

these species against the pressures of invasive exotics, disease, and other stresses. The river-valley and flood-plain networks provided many of the existing natural corridors. The protection and restoration of new natural corridors has been tempered by private ownership and agricultural production. As a result, governments have preferred incentives and, in some cases, like the Oak Ridges Moraine, special zoning to protect and encourage the restoration of natural connections.

Another dramatic technical development has been the application of Geographic Information Systems (GIS), software programs that allow conservation scientists to convert hard-to-visualize tables and numbers to maps. With GIS, conservation scientists can map and analyze the presence and abundance of habitats and creatures, producing information in vivid colours. Such visual representations advance understanding and help planners and the public understand information more easily. Bill Stephenson, then a scientist with Parks Canada, found seed funding and championed "The Big Picture," which used GIS to identify a complete system of cores and corridors for the entire Carolinian zone for use in municipal planning.

Satellites and Geographic Positioning Systems (GPS) helped as well, by locating features to within a few metres. Larry McGill, a progressive Carolinian farmer, used detailed grain-yield data linked to exact-location data from GPS on his combine to identify the best and poorest parts of his farm. He could then map the information using GIS. This showed which parts of his farm fields failed to yield an adequate return for his costly inputs, and which areas could be retired for nature without economic loss. Technology changed how conservation science looked at the land and greatly enhanced the ability to communicate that information to the public.

FIRST NATIONS

Maps and satellite imagery strikingly reveal the patchwork nature of Carolinian Canada. The region exists as a network of cities, towns, and cultivated fields, with few scattered patches of relatively intact natural areas remaining in the landscape. What maps also reveal, though, is that the largest of these natural areas are on First Nations land, and that they have been protected through decades of First Nations stewardship.

The largest single block of Carolinian woodland in Canada — visible even on a satellite image shot from hundreds of kilometres above the earth — exists on the Six Nations of the Grand River Territory. Roughly 45 percent of the Six Nation's forty-six-thousand-acre territory is covered in forests of oak, hickory, maple, walnut, and other hardwoods. Committed to preserving and enhancing the forest, the Eco-Centre at Six Nations is involved in a number of stewardship activities. One project in particular ensures that the next generation will continue the strong tradition of forest stewardship: school children nurture tree seedlings in school greenhouses until the trees are ready to be planted at restoration sites.

Nestled between Ontario and Michigan, at the mouth of the St. Clair River, Walpole Island First Nation supports some of the most biologically diverse natural areas remaining in Canada. It has one of the largest tracts of forest cover in southwestern Ontario, one of the largest wetland systems in the Great Lakes Basin, the most significant tallgrass prairie and oak savanna in Canada, and one of the highest numbers of rare species in the province. Any one of these features on its own would be of enormous significance; that these natural features persist is due to the stewardship of the Walpole Island First Nation, which is developing an ecosystem-based Recovery Strategy for the significant habitats and species under its care. A cornerstone principle of the recovery strategy is that humans are part of nature, so conservation needs to be tied to their culture: recovering species and spaces goes hand in hand with recovering a culture. The two are interconnected.

CONSERVATION ACTION IN THE FUTURE

In many ways, the conservation challenges in the Carolinian zone mirror the conservation challenges found everywhere in Canada. What is unique is that all of the threats — habitat loss and fragmentation, invasive exotic species, pollution, to name just the major ones — are combined and magnified in this relatively small region, home to approximately one-quarter of Canada's population, the industrial and agricultural heartland of the nation. This is one of the most threatened landscapes in North America, with multiple stresses overlapping in a region with so many special species and habitats.

One of the most profound changes to conservation in the Carolinian zone is the broad recognition that all conservation efforts, even those on a small scale, connect to the larger picture. Protection of individual species and preservation of specific sites will only work if the wider landscape functions as a network or web of intact, functioning ecosystems.

And the lesson of protection doesn't end there. The landscape of Carolinian Canada also depends on healthy communities — in the broadest sense. For conservation efforts to succeed, it is necessary to find sensible and fair economic solutions that support, for example, the farming community and sustainable rural communities.

While the challenges are enormous, there have been many successes in the conservation of Carolinian Canada over the past twenty years. Many of these relate to new policy: the development of land trusts and legislation to support them; planning initiatives by progressive municipalities that enshrine natural-heritage principles in Official Plans; legal tools such as conservation easements, and eco-friendly tax incentives, such as the Conservation Land Tax Incentive Program and the Ecological Gifts Program; changes to zoning laws and the provincial *Planning Act* that recognize and protect natural areas.

However, there is no "magic bullet" or "big fix" that will halt the loss of biodiversity and natural habitats. All levels of government — from municipal and regional to provincial and federal — must be engaged. And all citizens — from private landowners acting individually to non-profit groups working together — need to be involved.

While the names will change, the region will always need champions. It is their diversity, vision, passion, and effort that will drive conservation action in the future, and therein lies our best hope for the natural heritage of Carolinian Canada.

EMBRACE THE PAST, HELP SHAPE THE FUTURE

Gordon Nelson with Michelle Kanter

THE OUTSTANDING AND UNIQUE natural qualities of the Carolinian region are clear, as are the rising pressures on the region through continued growth of population, urban areas and sprawl, industrial agriculture, and other intensive land uses. The need for a strong commitment to conservation, especially in relation to threatened species and habitats, has never been more urgent. The Carolinian Canada Coalition has been working on this challenge for more than two decades, and some of the results of that effort are set forth in this book.

It is encouraging that efforts are increasingly being made to conserve Carolinian species and the fragmented and diminished habitats that ultimately support them. But much work still needs to be done. The creation of national and provincial parks along with other protected areas set up by Conservation Authorities and municipal governments has been a vital building block for the conservation of the natural legacy of the Carolinian region. More protected areas are still needed. Yet historically such areas have only ensured protection for a small part of the region. Even with improvements for some vital areas, this will likely remain the case in the future.

In recent decades, a necessary shift has occurred: there is now much greater emphasis on private stewardship. Farmers, rural citizens, and city dwellers alike have embraced the challenge of stewarding the species and habitats we all share. These enthusiastic participants in protection have contributed individually and through non-governmental organizations such as Conservation Authorities, the Nature Conservancy of Canada, and a growing number of land trusts.

Increasing numbers of landowners are helping to create natural heritage networks and signing conservation easements to protect pieces of their landscape forever. Municipalities are zoning natural heritage sites, enshrining protection in municipal planning policies. Farmers are balancing conservation action with sustainable agriculture, using Environmental Farm Plans.

The Carolinian Canada Coalition has played a major role in coordinating these efforts. The Coalition has been guided by a Management Committee consisting of representatives of key government and non-government agencies in the region and by its small staff, which serves as a key hub around which the efforts of many organizations and volunteers can be connected. The strength of the Coalition has been in its ability to bring many voices and actions together in a unified approach to the conservation challenges in the region. A major current example is the Woodland Recovery Program, which will do much to protect and restore many of the valued species and habitats described in this book.

The Coalition is now working to encourage wider and more intensive involvement by many individual stewards on the ground. With this in mind, the Coalition is moving from a Management Committee to a Board made up of private citizens as well as representatives from key agencies and organizations. The Coalition is also preparing a Strategic Plan, which will guide its work in cooperation with concerned people and groups for the next five years.

Current efforts are guided by the Big Picture, a concept map that looks at the whole Carolinian landscape and connects 140 core remnants together to create a "natural network." This vision, which has been endorsed by a multitude of organizations as a foundation for sustainability in the region, allows us to tackle the sometimes overwhelming task of conservation on an ever-changing, multi-use landscape. The Coalition plans to monitor, assess, and report on conservation successes across the Big Picture.

The Carolinian Canada Coalition is one of a few such collaborative initiatives in the world. But many more hands are needed to meet the major challenges of the region: climate change, continuing habitat loss, increasing numbers of species at risk, urban sprawl, degraded water quality, exotic species, and more. We hope that you will join us in protecting, sustaining, and stewarding this unique landscape — to the seventh generation! For more information about the coalition, visit www.carolinian.org.

GLOSSARY

biodiversity: the variability among living organisms, including the diversity that occurs within species, between species, and in ecosystems.

biomagnification: the concentration of toxins as they move up the food chain.

biomass: the mass of living organisms within a defined space.

biota: the living component of an ecosystem.

Carolinian species: a popular term that has evolved to indicate a species that is native to Canada, with the bulk of its Canadian population being restricted to the Carolinian zone. In this sense, Carolinian Canada is an important refuge for these species and they add to the biodiversity of the zone and help characterize the zone as unique. Many Carolinian species such as Tulip-tree and Virginia Opossum have a "southern affinity." Others are prairie species with a western affinity, or Great Lakes endemics that have a restricted distribution in Canada. It should be noted that "Carolinian species" are only part of Carolinian Canada's biodiversity and that all native species resident in the zone contribute to the region's diversity.

climax community: stable, self-perpetuating vegetation community that represents the final stage of succession.

critical habitat: the habitat necessary for the survival of a wildlife species.

ecoregion: an area characterized by a distinctive regional climate as expressed by vegetation.

ecosystem: an interdependent and dynamic system of living organisms, along with their physical and geographical environment.

endemic species: a species native and confined to a certain region; having comparatively restricted distribution.

exotic species: a species that did not originally occur in the areas in which it is now found, but that arrived as a direct or indirect result of human activity.

forb: a non-grass herbaceous (non-woody) wildflower.

habitat: the particular type of environment occupied by an individual species or species population.

indicator species: a (usually) plant species indicates an ecological condition.

indigenous species: a species native to a particular geographic region.

invasive exotic species: a non-native species that has moved into an area and reproduced so aggressively that it has replaced some of the original native species.

monoculture: the planting of a single crop.

native species: a species that existed in an area prior to European settlement.

range: the geographic limits of a species or group.

southern-affinity species: species with populations centred on the Eastern Deciduous Forest Region in the northeastern United States with the northern limits of their range in or near the Carolinian zone (although some species may range as far north as the southern extent of the Canadian Shield).

Carolinian Places to Visit

Essex County

Cedar Creek Conservation Area:
(519) 776-5209; www.erca.org
Devonwood Conservation Authority:
(519) 776-5209; www.erca.org
Fish Point Provincial Nature Reserve:
(519) 825-4659; www.ontarioparks.com
Hillman Marsh Conservation Area:
(519) 776-5209; www.erca.org
Holiday Beach Conservation Area:
(519) 736-3772; www.erca.org
Lighthouse Point Provincial Nature Reserve:
(519) 825-4659; www.ontarioparks.com
Ojibway Prairie Provincial Nature Reserve:
(519) 966-5852; www.ojibway.ca
Point Pelee National Park: (519) 322-2365;
www.pc.gc.ca/pn-np/on/pelee/index_e.asp
Stone Road Alvar Nature Reserve: (519) 724-2291;
www.ontarionature.org
Tallgrass Prairie Heritage Park, Black Oak
Heritage Park, and Ojibway Park:
(519) 966-5852; www.ojibway.ca

Regional Municipality of Chatham-Kent

Clear Creek Forest Nature Reserve: (519) 674-1750
Rondeau Provincial Park: (519) 674-1750;
www.rondeauprovincialpark.ca
Sinclair's Bush: (519) 354-7310;
www.lowerthames-conservation.on.ca
St. Clair National Wildlife Area: (519) 354-1418
Wheatley Provincial Park: (519) 825-4659;
www.ontarioparks.com

Lambton County

Bickford Oak Woods Conservation Reserve;
(519) 354-7340
Ipperwash Dunes and Swales Nature Reserve:
www.lambtonwildlife.com
Ipperwash Provincial Park: (519) 243-2220;
www.ontarioparks.com
Karner Blue Sanctuary:
www.lambtonwildlife.com
L Lake Conservation Area: (519) 235-2610;
www.abca.on.ca
Lambton County Heritage Forest:
www.lambtononline.com
Pinery Provincial Park: (519) 243-2220;
www.pinerypark.on.ca
Port Franks Forested Dunes Nature Reserve:
www.lambtonwildlife.com
Rock Glen Conservation Area: (519) 828-3071;
www.abca.on.ca
Walpole Island First Nation: (519) 627-1475;
www.bkejwanong.com

Elgin County

Dutton-Dunwich Prairie:
www.naturallyelgin.org/duttonprairie.shtml
Port Burwell Provincial Park: (519) 874-4691;
www.ontarioparks.com
Springwater Forest: (519) 773-9037;
www.catfishcreek.ca

Middlesex County

Dorchester Swamp: (519) 451-2800;
www.thamesriver.on.ca
Komoka Provincial Park: (519) 874-4691;
www.ontarioparks.com
Longwoods Conservation Area: (519) 264-2420;
www.lowerthames-conservation.on.ca
Sifton Bog Natural Area: (519) 451-2800;
www.thamesriver.on.ca
Skunk's Misery: (519) 354-7310;
www.lowerthames-conservation.on.ca

Oxford County

Embro Upland Forest: (519) 451-2800;
www.thamesriver.on.ca
Lawson Nature Reserve: (416) 441-8419;
www.ontarionature.org
Trillium Woods Provincial Nature Reserve:
(519) 874-4691; www.ontarioparks.com

NORFOLK COUNTY

Backus Woods and Heritage Conservation Area:
(519) 586-2201; www.lprca.on.ca
Long Point Provincial Park: (519) 586-2133;
www.ontarioparks.com
St. Williams Conservation Reserve: (519) 773-9241
South Walsingham Sand Ridges: (519) 428-4623;
www.lprca.on.ca
Spooky Hollow Nature Sanctuary: (905) 381-0329;
www.hamiltonnature.org
Turkey Point Provincial Park: (519) 426-3239;
www.ontarioparks.com
Walsh Forest Complex: (519) 428-4623;
www.lprca.on.ca

HALDIMAND COUNTY

Ruthven Park: (905) 772-0560;
www.ruthvenpark.ca
Selkirk Provincial Park: (905) 776-2600;
www.ontarioparks.com

BRANT COUNTY

Gordon Glaves Memorial Pathway:
(519) 759-4150; www.city.brantford.on.ca
Grand River Rail Trail: (519) 621-2761;
www.grandriver.ca
Pinehurst Lake Conservation Area: (519) 442-4721;
www.grandriver.ca
Six Nations of the Grand River Territory:
(519) 445-0330; www.sixnations.ca

WATERLOO

F.W.R. Dickson Wilderness Area: (519) 442-4721;
www.grandriver.ca

NIAGARA

Ball's Falls Heritage Conservation Area:
(905) 788-3135; www.conservationniagara.on.ca
Beamer Memorial Conservation Area:
(905) 788-3135; www.conservation-
niagara.on.ca
Harold Mitchell Nature Reserve: (416) 441-8419;
www.ontarionature.org
Niagara Glen Nature Reserve: (905) 356-2241;
www.niagaraparks.com

Ruigrok Tract Conservation Area: (905) 788-3135;
www.conservation-niagara.on.ca
Short Hills Nature Sanctuary: (905) 381-0329;
www.hamiltonnature.org
Short Hills Provincial Park: (905) 774-6642;
www.ontarioparks.com
St. Johns Conservation Area: (905) 788-3135;
www.conservation-niagara.on.ca
Wainfleet Bog Conservation Area: (905) 788-3135;
www.conservation-niagara.on.ca
Willoughby Marsh Conservation Area:
(905) 788-3135; www.conservation-
niagara.on.ca

HAMILTON

Beverly Swamp: (905) 525-2181;
www.conservationhamilton.ca
Borer's Falls: (905) 527-1158; www.rbg.ca
Cartwright Nature Sanctuary: (905) 381-0329;
www.hamiltonnature.org
Cootes Paradise: (905) 527-1158; www.rbg.ca
Dundas Valley: (905) 627-1233;
www.conservationhamilton.ca
Rock Chapel: (905) 527-1158; www.rbg.ca
Spencer Gorge Conservation Area: (905) 628-3060;
www.conservationhamilton.ca

HALTON

Bronte Creek Provincial Park: (905) 827-6911;
www.ontarioparks.com
Iroquois Shoreline Woods: (905) 845-6601,
ext. 3076; www.oakville.ca
Mount Nemo Conservation Area: (905) 336-1158;
www.conservationhalton.on.ca
Waterdown Escarpment Woods: (905) 336-1158;
www.conservationhalton.on.ca

CITY OF TORONTO

High Park: (416) 392-1111; www.toronto.ca/park
Rouge Park: (905) 713-6038; www.rougepark.com

FURTHER READING AND SOURCES

GENERAL

Aboud, S., and Henry Kock. *A Life Zone Approach to School Yard Naturalization: The Carolinian Life Zone.* Guelph: University of Guelph Arboretum, 1994.

Allen, G. M.; P. F. J. Eagles; and S. D. Price (eds.). *Conserving Carolinian Canada.* Waterloo: University of Waterloo Press, 1990.

Argus, G. W., et al. *Atlas of the Rare Vascular Plants of Ontario.* (Four Parts). Ottawa: National Museum of Natural Sciences, 1982-1987.

Beechey, Tom J.; George R. Francis; and Dianne M. Powell (eds.). *Caring for Southern Remnants: Special Species, Special Spaces.* Ottawa: Canadian Council on Ecological Areas, 1999.

Brownell, V., and J. L. Riley. *The Alvars of Ontario.* Don Mills: Federation of Ontario Naturalists, 2000.

Celestino, M. *Wildflowers of the Canadian Erie Islands.* Windsor: Essex County Field Naturalists, 2002.

Chapman, L. J., and D. F. Putnam. *The Physiography of Southern Ontario.* Toronto: University of Toronto Press, 1951.

Cundiff, Brad. *The Hike Ontario Guide to Walks in Carolinian Canada.* Erin, Ont.: Boston Mills Press, 1998.

Dickinson, Timothy, et al. *The ROM Field Guide to Wildflowers of Ontario.* Toronto: Royal Ontario Museum and McClelland & Stewart Ltd., 2004.

Eagles, P. F. J., and T. J. Beechey. *Critical Unprotected Natural Areas of the Carolinian Life Zone of Canada.* Toronto: Nature Conservancy of Canada, Ontario Heritage Foundation and World Wildlife Fund, 1985.

Explore Our Natural World: A Biodiversity Atlas of the Lake Huron to Lake Erie Corridor. Wildlife Habitat Council's Great Lakes Regional Office, 2004.

Federation of Ontario Naturalists (FON). *Seasons.* Summer issue, 1985.

Johnson, Lorraine. *Carolinian Canada Signature Sites.* London, Ontario: Carolinian Canada Coalition, 2005.

Lamb, Larry, and Gail Rhynard. *Plants of Carolinian Canada.* Don Mills: Federation of Ontario Naturalists, 1994.

Theberge, J. B. (ed.). *Legacy: The Natural History of Ontario.* Toronto: McClelland & Stewart, 1989.

Wake, Winnifred (ed.). *A Nature Guide to Ontario.* Toronto: University of Toronto Press, 1997.

CHAPTER 1

Armson, K. A. *Ontario's Forests: A Historical Perspective.* Toronto: Fitzhenry & Whiteside and Ontario Forestry Association, 2001.

Barron, George. *Mushrooms of Ontario & Eastern Canada.* Edmonton: Lone Pine, 1999.

Cox, Donald. *A Naturalist's Guide to Forest Plants: An Ecology for Eastern North America.* Syracuse, N.Y.: Syracuse University Press, 2003.

Kricher, John C. *A Field Guide to Eastern Forests, North America.* Boston: Houghton Miflin, 1988.

Larson, B. M., et al. *Woodland Heritage of Southern Ontario.* Don Mills: Federation of Ontario Naturalists, 1999.

Peterson, Roger Tory, and Margaret McKenny. *A Field Guide to Wildflowers: Northeastern and North-Central North America.* Boston: Houghton Mifflin, 1996.

Soper, James. H., and Margaret L. Heimburger. *Shrubs of Ontario.* Toronto: Royal Ontario Museum, 1994.

Waldron, Gerry. *Trees of the Carolinian Forest: A Guide to Species, Their Ecology and Uses.* Erin: Boston Mills Press, 2003.

CHAPTER 2

Delaney, Kim, et al. *Planting the Seed: A Guide to Establishing Prairie and Meadow Communities in Southern Ontario.*
Burlington: Environment Canada, 2000.

Madson, J. *Tallgrass Prairie.* Billings, MT: Falcon Press in cooperation with The Nature Conservancy, 1993.

Madson, J. *Where the Sky Began: Land of the Tallgrass Prairie.* Boston: Houghton Mifflin, 1982.

Packard, S., and C.F. Mutel, (eds.). *The Tallgrass Restoration Handbook for Prairies, Savannas and Woodlands.* Washington, DC: Island Press, 1997.

Rodger, Lindsay. *Tallgrass Communities of Southern Ontario: A Recovery Plan.* Toronto: Ministry of Natural Resources and World Wildlife Fund, 1998.

Wickett, R. G., P .D. Lewis, A. Woodliffe, and P. Pratt, (eds.). *Proceedings of the Thirteenth North American Prairie Conference.* 1994. (Available from Department of Parks and Recreation, 2450 McDougall Avenue, Windsor, ON N8X 3N6.)

CHAPTER 3

Cox, Donald. *A Naturalist's Guide to Wetland Plants: An ecology for eastern North America.* Syracuse, N.Y.: Syracuse University Press, 2002.

Cronk, J. K. *Wetland Plants.* Stockport, England: Lewis Publishers, 2001.

Crow, Garrett E. *Aquatic and Wetland Plants of Northeastern North America.* Madison: University of Wisconsin Press, 2000.

Keddy, Paul A. *Wetland Ecology: Principles and Conservation.* New York: Cambridge University Press, 2000.

Mitsch, William J. *Wetlands.* New York: John Wiley, 2000.

The Ontario Great Lakes Coastal Wetland Atlas: A Summary of Information (1983-1997). Environment Canada, Ontario Ministry of Natural Resources, and Natural Heritage Information Centre, 2003.

CHAPTER 4

Banfield, A. W. F. *The Mammals of Canada.* Toronto: University of Toronto Press, 1974.

Dobbyn, J. S. *Atlas of the Mammals of Ontario.* Don Mills: Federation of Ontario Naturalists, 1994. (Out of print but currently available for download from the Ontario Nature website, www.ontarionature.org.)

Kurta, A. *Mammals of the Great Lakes Region.* Markham: Fitzhenry & Whiteside Ltd., 1995.

Peterson, R. L. *The Mammals of Eastern Canada.* Toronto: Oxford University Press, 1966.

Van Zyll de Jong, C. G. *Handbook of Canadian Mammals.* 1. *Marsupials and Insectivores.* Ottawa: National Museum of Natural Sciences, 1983. (Available from the Canadian Museum of Nature at www.nature.ca/nature_e.cfm.)

_____. *Handbook of Canadian Mammals.* 2. *Bats.* Ottawa: National Museum of Natural Sciences, 1985. (Available from the Canadian Museum of Nature at http://www.nature.ca/nature_e.cfm.)

Vlasman, K. *Atlas of the Mammals of Hamilton.* Hamilton: The Hamilton Conservation Authority, 2005. (Available from the Hamilton Naturalists' Club: www.hamiltonnature.org.)

CHAPTER 5

Cadman, M. D., P. F. J. Eagles, and F. M. Helleiner. *Atlas of the Breeding Birds of Ontario.* Waterloo: University of Waterloo Press, 1987.

Fisher, Chris. *Ontario Birds: A Field Guide to 125 Common Birds of Ontario.* Edmonton: Lone Pine, 1996.

Hughes, Janice M. *The ROM Field Guide to Birds of Ontario.* Toronto: Royal Ontario Museum and McClelland & Stewart, 2001.

Peterson, Roger Tory. *A Field Guide to the Birds: A Completely New Guide to All the Birds of Eastern and Central North America.* Boston: Houghton Mifflin, 1980.

Sibley, David. *Field Guide to the Birds of Eastern North America.* London: Christopher Helm, 2003.

CHAPTER 6

Cook, F. R. *Introduction to Canadian Amphibians and Reptiles.* Ottawa: National Museum of Natural Sciences, 1984.

Harding, J. H. *Amphibians and Reptiles of the Great Lakes Region.* Ann Arbor: University of Michigan Press, 1997.

Johnson, Bob. *Familiar Amphibians and Reptiles of Ontario.* Toronto: Natural Heritage/Natural History, 1989.

Lamond, W. G. *The Reptiles and Amphibians of the Hamilton Area: An Historical Summary and the Results of the Hamilton Herpetofaunal Atlas.* Hamilton: Hamilton Naturalists' Club, 1994.

MacCulloch, R. D. *The ROM Field Guide to Amphibians and Reptiles of Ontario.* Toronto: Royal Ontario Museum and McClelland & Stewart Ltd., 2002.

Marshall, Stephen A. *Insects: Their Natural History and Diversity with a Photographic Guide to Insects of Eastern North America.* Toronto: Firefly Books, 2006.

Oldham, M. J., and W. F. Weller. *Ontario Herpetofaunal Atlas.* Peterborough: Natural Heritage Information Centre, 2000.

CHAPTER 7

Hubbs, Carl L. (revised by Gerald R. Smith). *Fishes of the Great Lakes Region.* Ann Arbor, Michigan: University of Michigan, 2004.

Metcalfe-Smith, J., et al. *Photo Field Guide to the Freshwater Mussels of Ontario.* St. Thomas: St. Thomas Field Naturalists, 2006.

Scott, W. B. *Fishes of Canada.* Oakville, Ontario: Galt House Publications, 1998.

CHAPTER 8

Borror, Donald J., and Richard E. White. *A Field Guide to Insects: America North of Mexico.* Boston: Houghton Mifflin, 1998.

Carmichael, I., and A. Vance. *Photo Field Guide to the Butterflies of Southern Ontario.* St. Thomas: St. Thomas Field Naturalists, 2003.

Carmichael, I., and A. Vance. *Photo Field Guide to the Caterpillars of Southern Ontario.* St. Thomas: St. Thomas Field Naturalists, 2004.

Carmichael, I., A. MacKenzie, and B. Steinberg. *Photo Field Guide to the Dragonflies of Southwestern Ontario.* St. Thomas: St. Thomas Field Naturalists, 2002.

Holmes, Anthony M., et al. *The Ontario Butterfly Atlas.* Toronto: Toronto Entomologists' Association, 1991.

Opler, Paul A. *Peterson Field Guide to Butterflies and Moths.* Boston: Houghton Mifflin, 1994.

CHAPTER 9

Clarke, John. *Land, Power, and Economics on the Frontier of Upper Canada.* Montreal/Kingston: McGill-Queen's University Press, 2001.

Ellis, Chris, and Neal Ferris (eds.). *The Archaeology of Southern Ontario to AD 1650.* London, Ontario, 1990. Occasional Publication of the London Chapter Ontario Archaeological Society Number 5.

Finlayson, William David, et al. *London, Ontario: The First 11,000 Years.* London, Ontario: Museum of Indian Archaeology, 1990.

Gentilcore, R. Louis, and Geoffrey Matthews (eds). *Historical Atlas of Canada. Volume 2: The Land Transformed, 1800-1891.* Toronto: University of Toronto Press, 1993.

Harris, R. Cole, and Geoffrey Matthews (eds.). *Historical Atlas of Canada. Volume 1: From the Beginning to 1800.* Toronto: University of Toronto Press, 1987.

R. Cole Harris, and John Warkentin. *Canada before Confederation.* Toronto: Oxford University Press, 1974.

Jones, Robert L. *History of Agriculture in Ontario, 1613 – 1880.* Toronto: University of Toronto Press, 1946.

Kelly, Kenneth. "The Changing Attitude of Farmers to Forest in Nineteenth-Century Ontario." *Ontario Geography* 8 (1974): 64-77.

McIlwraith, Thomas. *Looking for Old Ontario.* Toronto: University of Toronto Press, 1997.

Martin, Virgil. *The Changing Landscape of Ontario.* Erin, Ontario: Boston Mills Press, 1988.

Nelson, J. Gordon, et al. *The Grand River Watershed: A Heritage Landscape Guide.* Heritage Landscape Guide Series #2. Waterloo: Heritage Resources Centre, University of Waterloo, 2003.

Riley, John L., and Pat Mohr. *The Natural Heritage of Southern Ontario's Settled Landscapes.* Aurora: Ministry of Natural Resources, 1994.

Thames River Background Study Research Team. *Background Study: Thames River Watershed, Ontario.* London: Upper Thames River Conservation Authority, 1998.

Wood, J. David. *Making Ontario: Agricultural Colonization and Landscape Re-creation before the Railway.* Montreal/Kingston: McGill-Queen's University Press, 2000.

CHAPTER 10

Daigle, J-M, and D. Havinga. *Restoring Nature's Place: A Guide to Naturalizing Ontario Parks and Greenspace.* Schomberg: Ecological Outlook Consulting and Ontario Parks Association, 1996.

Hilts, S., and P. Mitchell. *Caring for Your Land: A Stewardship Handbook for Carolinian Canada Landowners.* Guelph: Centre for Land and Water Stewardship, 1998.

Hilts, Stewart, and Ron Reid. *Creative Conservation: A Handbook for Ontario Land Trusts.* Don Mills: Federation of Ontario Naturalists, 1994.

Hilts, Stewart, et al (eds.). *Islands of Green: Natural Heritage Protection in Ontario.* Toronto: Ontario Heritage Foundation, 1986.

Hilts, Stewart, and T. Moull. *Protecting Ontario's Natural Heritage Through Private Stewardship.* Toronto: Natural Heritage League, 1985.

Johnson, Lorraine. *The New Ontario Naturalized Garden.* Vancouver: Whitecap Books, 2001.

Killan, Gerald. *Protected Places: A History of Ontario's Provincial Parks System.* Toronto: Dundurn Press, 1993.

Labatt, Lori, and Bruce Litteljohn (eds). *Islands of Hope: Ontario's Parks and Wilderness.* Willowdale, Ontario: Firefly, 1992.

ORGANIZATIONS AND WEB SOURCES

American Society of Mammalogists: http://timssnet.allenpress.com/ECOMASMM/timssnet/common/tnt_frontpage.cfm

Bird Studies Canada: www.bsc-eoc.org

Canadian Amphibian and Reptile Conservation Network: www.carcnet.ca

Canadian Council of Ecological Areas: www.ccea.org

Carolinian Canada Coalition: www.carolinian.org

Committee on the Status of Endangered Wildlife in Canada (COSEWIC): www.cosewic.gc.ca

Committee on the Status of Species at Risk in Ontario: www.ontarioparks.com/english/sar.html or www.rom.on.ca/ontario/risk.php

National Museum of Natural Sciences: www.mnh2.si.edu/education/mna

Natural Heritage Information Centre: www.mnr.gov.on.ca/MNR/nhic/nhic.html

Nature Conservancy of Canada: www.natureconservancy.ca

Ontario Land Trust Alliance: www.ontariolandtrustalliance.org

Ontario Nature: www.ontarionature.org

Ontario Stewardship Councils: www.ontariostewardship.org

Parks Research Forum of Ontario: www.prfo.ca

Society for Ecological Restoration: www.serontario.org

Tallgrass Ontario: www.tallgrassontario.org

Wildspace: www.on.ec.gc.ca/wildlife/wildspace/intro-e.html

World Wildlife Fund Canada: www.wwfcanada.org

CONTRIBUTORS' BIOGRAPHIES

Wasyl Bakowsky is a vegetation ecologist with the Natural Heritage Information Centre (NHIC), Ontario Ministry of Natural Resources. He studies and records information on significant plants and plant communities in Ontario. He has a Master's degree from the University of Toronto, where he focused on oak savanna vegetation in the southern part of the province. Prior to joining NHIC, he worked as a botanist for a consulting firm.

Gregor Beck is a wildlife biologist and environmental educator with degrees in biology (B.Sc., Guelph; M.Sc., McGill) and education (B.Ed., St. Francis Xavier). He has directed conservation and science programs with Bird Studies Canada, Ontario Nature, and QLF/Atlantic Centre for the Environment, taught at Ryerson University and Seneca College, and conducted research for Fisheries and Oceans Canada. He is author of *Watersheds: A Practical Handbook for Healthy Water* and co-editor of *Voices for the Watershed*. Gregor is a keen naturalist and has worked in some of Canada's more remote corners. He now resides in the heart of Carolinian Canada, overlooking Lake Erie, amidst woodlands, marshes, and ravines.

Tom Beechey is one of the founders of the Carolinian Canada Program and has assisted with many aspects of its work, including procurement of provincial funding, evaluation of sites for protection, the setting of land-acquisition priorities, and the development of private stewardship initiatives. Since retiring in 2001 as the Senior Conservation Biologist with Ontario Parks, he continues to be involved with many initiatives dealing with protected areas and biodiversity conservation. He remains active as an associate director of the Canadian Council on Ecological Areas, serves on the Ontario board of the Nature Conservancy of Canada, and participates on the steering committee of Parks Research Forum of Ontario. Related pursuits include travelling, natural-history study, and nature photography.

Alan Dextrase has a Bachelor of Science from the University of Guelph and a Master's of Science from Lakehead University. He worked as a fisheries biologist with the Ontario Ministry of Natural Resources in northwestern Ontario from 1985 to 1993. For the past thirteen years, Alan has been employed as a senior biologist with the OMNR in Peterborough, where he has worked on policy and management issues related to non-indigenous species and aquatic species at risk. He is a member of COSEWIC, participates on several recovery teams for aquatic species at risk, and is currently pursuing a Ph.D. at Trent University.

William DeYoung is a landscape ecologist who has lived in London for the past twenty-five years. Bill has a passion for learning and a keen desire to share this knowledge with others through his work and volunteer activities, for which he has won several awards. He studied biology and geography at Trent University and sociology at King's College. Bill's most recent achievement is the completion of a post-graduate degree from the University of Western Ontario. His research used LANDSAT satellite imagery in an evaluation model to identify woodlands and wildlife habitat for conservation priority ranking in southern Ontario. When not doing statistical survey work, you can always find Bill designing ecological landscapes for another ReForest London project to improve London's tree cover. His avocation is to promote conservation; he does this through the Thames Talbot Land Trust and other volunteer organizations.

Sandy Dobbyn has had an interest in mammals for as long as he can remember. After graduating from the University of Guelph, he coordinated the Ontario Mammal Atlas project for the Federation of Ontario Naturalists (now Ontario Nature), and eventually published the *Atlas of the Mammals of Ontario*, which is the most up-to-date publication on the distribution of mammals in the province. Sandy has been working in the Carolinian zone since 1997, when he began doing field work for Bird Studies Canada on the endangered Prothonotary Warbler. That work exposed him to many of the Carolinian gems along the north shore of Lake Erie, and particularly Rondeau Provincial Park, where he eventually became the Park Naturalist. Currently Sandy is the Zone Ecologist for the southwest zone of Ontario Parks in London, where he continues to work to preserve and restore Carolinian habitats.

Lorraine Johnson is the author of many books related to native plant gardening, including *100 Easy-to-Grow Native Plants* and *The New Ontario Naturalized Garden*. She is past president of the North American Native Plant Society, and frequently lectures on environmental landscaping. Lorraine credits Larry Lamb and Gail Rhynard with introducing her to the plants of Carolinian Canada a decade ago, and thanks Mary Gartshore and Peter Carson for nurturing that interest over the years.

Michelle Kanter has held the position of Executive Director of the Carolinian Canada Coalition since 2003. Her work with the Coalition dates back to 1985 when she was first involved in landowner contact at Carolinian Canada Signature Sites. She studied at the University of Guelph, and has worked as a wildlife biologist in Carolinian Canada, northern Australia, and Canada's high Arctic. Her focus evolved to community stewardship, working closely with landowners, municipalities, and local groups to protect natural heritage. As a consultant, she developed an award-winning program and, at the Nature Conservancy of Canada, she helped protect some of the best remaining natural areas in the Carolinian life zone.

Kevin Kavanagh (B.Sc.-Hons., McGill; M.Sc., York) has worked in the field of conservation for most of his professional life. He is currently the National Manager of Land Stewardship for the Nature Conservancy of Canada. Prior to this, he spent fifteen years with World Wildlife Fund Canada, where he worked on protected-areas planning and the recovery of species at risk. Kevin is a past president of the Canadian Parks and Wilderness Society — Wildlands League chapter, and has served on the boards of several other conservation organizations over the past twenty-five years. An avid gardener and bird-watcher, Kevin believes these interests were instilled in him at an early age while he was growing up surrounded by nature in Quebec's Eastern Townships. He now resides in Carolinian Canada, where he is indulging his passion for forest restoration and gardening with plants from the "deep south."

Jon McCracken jokes that he has been "studying birds since I was knee-high to a Grasshopper Sparrow." After graduating with an honours B.Sc. in Zoology from the University of Western Ontario, and having gained several years of invaluable mentoring at Long Point Bird Observatory, he worked for twelve years as a contract biologist for government agencies, non-governmental organizations, and industry. He returned "home" in 1989, joining the talented staff of Bird Studies Canada (formerly Long Point Bird Observatory), where he is the organization's senior Program Manager, responsible for designing and overseeing a wide variety of ornithological research and conservation programs locally, provincially, nationally, and internationally. Over the years, his work has taken him from high Arctic polar deserts to steamy jungles, but he is the first to admit to feeling most at home exploring (and still discovering) the heart, soul, and condition of Carolinian Canada's forests, marshes, and swamps.

Deborah Metsger has been Assistant Curator of Botany at the Royal Ontario Museum (ROM) since 1982. She is responsible for the management of the ROM'S Green Plant Herbarium and is co-editor of the book *Managing the Modern Herbarium* (Metsger and Byers, 1999). She has conducted floristic investigations throughout Ontario and is a co-author of *The ROM Field Guide to the Wildflowers of Ontario*, published by the ROM and McClelland & Stewart in 2004. She has participated in a long-term study of the aquatic ecosystems of Walpole Island First Nation and has collaborated with the Walpole Island Heritage Centre on numerous projects and committees. Deborah has been extensively involved in the development of several ROM galleries and exhibits, including the Hands-on Biodiversity Gallery, and has conducted numerous public programs and lectures.

Gordon Nelson is a Distinguished Professor Emeritus at the University of Waterloo and a former Dean of the Faculty of Environmental Studies at that university. He is currently Chair of the Carolinian Canada Coalition and also Parks Research Forum of Ontario. He is especially interested in land use, landscape and environmental planning and decision making, and is the author of numerous publications. These include *Towards a Grand Sense of Place* (2004); *Towards a Sense of Place: Preparing Heritage Landscape Guides, A Manual for Urban and Rural Communities in Ontario* (2005); and *Protected Areas and the Regional Planning Imperative: Integrating Nature Conservation and Sustainable Development* (2003).

Michael J. Oldham is Botanist/Herpetologist with Ontario's Natural Heritage Information Centre in Peterborough, a position he has held for eleven years. Previously he worked as an MNR District Ecologist and Assistant Regional Ecologist. Before coming to MNR, he spent six years as staff biologist for the Essex Region Conservation Authority. He graduated from the University of Guelph in 1980, and has diverse natural-history and conservation-biology interests. A passion for fieldwork has led Mike to explore many of Ontario's natural areas, resulting in the discovery of several dozen plant species not previously known from the province and numerous range extensions.

Paul Pratt has worked as the Naturalist for the City of Windsor since 1975. He manages the Ojibway Nature Centre and the parks that make up the nationally significant Ojibway Prairie Complex. He has written extensively on tallgrass prairie and various aspects of natural history, including insects. Paul is a co-editor of *Ontario Odonata* and has discovered several dragonflies new to Canada in recent years.

Steven Price is Senior Conservation Director for World Wildlife Fund-Canada, responsible for a team addressing a range of conservation issues in Canada and abroad, including climate change, marine, forests, freshwater, toxics, and species conservation. Having served at WWF–Canada for more than twenty-five years, Steven's first major conservation program was the Carolinian Canada Coalition, which he helped conceive and lead. Steven has also helped develop the Forest Stewardship Council in Canada, as well as WWF's conservation program in Latin America and endangered-species projects in Canada. He holds a Bachelor's degree in Zoology and a Master's degree in Botany, both from the University of Toronto.

Shawn Staton holds an Honours B.Sc. in Biology from the University of Guelph and has been working as an aquatic biologist for more than ten years. He has been employed by several organizations, including private consulting firms, the Hamilton Region Conservation Authority, Environment Canada, and most recently the Department of Fisheries and Oceans. Shawn has a passionate interest in freshwater conservation and is currently involved in recovery planning for fish and mussel species at risk.

Ric Symmes has been involved with natural heritage conservation for thirty-five years. He is co-author (with Ron Reid and Doug van Hemessen) of *A Conservation Strategy for Carolinian Canada*, and served as Chair of the Carolinian Canada Coalition in 1998. When he was Executive Director of the Federation of Ontario Naturalists, he was involved with the creation of 378 new parks under the Ontario Forest Accord and creation of the Oak Ridges Moraine Act and Plan in 2001. Until recently he worked for the Nature Conservancy of Canada, Georgian Bay–Huronia region. He volunteers as vice-chair of the Ontario Parks Board and as a director at the Oak Ridges Moraine Foundation.

Michael Troughton (1939–2007), Emeritus Professor, Department of Geography, University of Western Ontario, had a long-term research and teaching interest in the cultural (rural, agricultural, and historical) geography of Canada, including an emphasis on southern Ontario. The author of several books and many articles and book chapters, he helped to compile the *Background Study of the Thames River Watershed and Nomination Proposal*, which led to the designation of the Thames as a Canadian Heritage River (2000). He was chair of the Thames Canadian Heritage River Committee and a member of the Middlesex Stewardship Committee.

Allen Woodliffe grew up in the heart of the Carolinian zone, just outside Rondeau Provincial Park, where he first began discovering and photographing the flora and fauna of Ontario. This led to a biology degree from the University of Guelph and, from 1973 to 1985, a position as Park Naturalist at Rondeau. Since 1985, he has been the District Ecologist for the former Chatham District and currently for the expanded Aylmer District (OMNR), which occupies at least 80 percent of the Carolinian zone. The ecology of prairie, savanna, woodlands, wetlands, and species at risk, along with photography and writing, have been his focus ever since.

ACKNOWLEDGEMENTS

THIS BOOK HAS BEEN a labour of love for the many people who contributed text and images, and for the dozens more who offered advice, encouragement, and feedback throughout the long process of transforming a seedling idea into reality. At every stage, these Carolinian experts with a passion for the region responded cheerfully and speedily to the editor's many queries and requests for assistance.

With deep gratitude, the editor would like to thank Daniel Kraus of the Nature Conservancy of Canada for directing the seed of an idea to fertile soil; Michelle Kanter, Executive Director of the Carolinian Canada Coalition, for her incisive and gracious collaboration at every stage; John Ambrose, Michelle Kanter, Daniel Kraus, Gordon Nelson, and Heather Webb of the Carolinian Canada Book Committee for guidance, expert opinions, and correction when necessary throughout the development of this book, and helpful comments on the manuscript; and James Wagar for handling the coordination of the photo database efficiently and with good humour.

Many people graciously offered ideas, advice, and assistance. The editor thanks Peter Banks, Tom Beechey, Jane Bowles, Michael Bradstreet, Graham Bryan, Christine Elliott, Mary Gartshore, Paul General, Ron Gould, Larry Lamb, Dave Martin, Nikki May, Vicki McKay, Mathis Natvik, Nancy Patterson, Ben Porchuk, Lindsay Rodger, Paul Smith, Mark Stabb, Bill Stephenson, Dorothy Tiedje, Ron Tiessen, Cheryl Veary, Winnie Wake, Gerry Waldron, and Will Wilson for their generous input to the project.

Along with the Carolinian Canada Book Committee, many people reviewed various sections of the manuscript and provided frank, insightful, and helpful comments: Gregor Beck, Graham Bryan, Stan Caveney, Sandy Dobbyn, Paul General, Scott Gillingwater, Clint Jacobs, Michelle Kanter, Donald Kirk, Don Lafontaine, Larry Lamb, Dale Leadbeater, Nick Mandrak, Dave Martin, Peter Mitchell, David Morris, Todd Morris, Gordon Nelson, Ben Porchuk, Julie Rosenthal, Janice Smith, Don Sutherland, Ron Tasker, and Will Wilson. The editor offers thanks, along with the usual caveat that any deficiencies that remain are not the responsibility of reviewers or advisors.

Finally, it is to the contributing authors and photographers that the most heartfelt cheer should go. It was a pleasure and an honour to work with you. Many, many thanks.

Not only did all of the people acknowledged above make this book possible — through their efforts, and in a myriad of ways, they are inspirational champions of the Carolinian zone and of the need to protect and restore it.

For photo assistance, the editor would like to thank Barry Arnott, Cindy Barrett, Gera Dillon, Shanna Dunlop, Kevin Railsback, Ron Ridout, John Schwindt, Janice Smith, Katie Stammler, Joseph Tomelleri, Robert Tremain, Doug van Hemessen, and Ed Woltmann.

The editor wishes to thank family and friends, in particular Ross Johnson, Linda Gustafson, and Andrew Leyerle, for their support.

— Lorraine Johnson, Editor

THE CAROLINIAN CANADA COALITION is thankful to our volunteers, members, staff, and generous supporters and sponsors who have helped to protect the unique nature of southwestern Ontario and celebrate it in this book.

In particular, the Nature Conservancy of Canada provided financial support for this project. The George Cedric Metcalf Charitable Foundation supported our Big Picture Communications Strategy that helped seed this book.

Our chair, Dr. Gordon Nelson, assisted with vision and patience, and the members of the CCC Management Committee provided strong moral support and guidance.

At the heart of this book is editor Lorraine Johnson, whose dedication, both as a consultant and volunteer, nurtured and shaped this book through many challenges to vividly capture the passion we all feel for this region.

— Michelle Kanter, Executive Director, Carolinian Canada Coalition

THIS IS A MONUMENTAL PROJECT for the Carolinian Canada Coalition. It represents a major effort to describe and portray the special nature of Carolinian Canada to people who live in and outside the region. Many of those who contributed have been recognized by Lorraine Johnson and Michelle Kanter. It should also be clear that without the skillful and dedicated persistence of these two leaders in preparing this book, it would not now be here for all to enjoy. We owe Lorraine Johnson and Michelle Kanter a great debt.

— Gordon Nelson, Chair, Carolinian Canada Coalition

INDEX

Page numbers in italics refer to illustrations.

a

Admiral, Red, 111
agriculture, 13
   history of, 125-126
Alumroot, 44
alvars, 43-45
Ambystoma, 89-90
American War of
   Independence, 127
Ancaster Creek, 124
Anemone, Canada, 41
anthracnose, 31
Archaic period, 125
Ash, Blue, 31
Ash, Pumpkin, 12, *12*, 31
Ash, White, 42
Aspen, 42
Aspen, Quaking, 12
Aster, Flat-topped, 42
Aster, Hairy, 42
Aster, Heath, 42
Aster, New England, 42
Aster, Sky Blue, 42
Attawandron, 126
Ausable River, 104, 108
Ausable River, Old, *127*

b

Backus Woods, 16, 86
Badger, 70-71
Bass, Largemouth, 102-103
Bass, Smallmouth,
   102-103, 104
Bat, Little Brown, 67, *72*
Bayly, "Terk", 139
Bear, Black, 13, 64
Beard-tongue, Hairy, 41
Beard-tongue, Smooth, 41
Beech, American, *15*, 23,
   24, 26, 31
beech-maple forest, 39
Bergamot, Wild, 41
Beverley Swamp, *47*
Big Picture, ecological
   vision, 122-123, 144, 148
Biosphere Reserve, 60
Birch, Paper, 12
Birch, Yellow, 27
Bird Studies Canada, 98
bison, 38
Bittern, Least, 85
Bittersweet, Oriental, 32
Black Sandshell, *101*
Blackbird, Red-winged, 9-
   10, *86*

Black-eyed Susan, 41
Blazing Star, *38*, 135
Blazing-star, Dense, 42
Bloodroot, *33*
Blue Pickerel. *See* Pike,
   Blue
Blue Walleye, 15. *See also*
   Pike, Blue
Blueberry, Highbush, 30, 56
Bluebird, Eastern, *74*
Blue-eyed Grass, 41
Bluestem, Big, 40, *40*, 135
Bluestem, Little, 40, *40*
Bobcat, 62, 64
Bobolink, 84
Bobwhite, Northern, 62,
   80, 84
Bog-rosemary, 56
Bothwell Sand Plain, 70
Bottlebrush Grass, 40
Bronte Provincial Park, 16
Bruce Peninsula, 45
Buckeye, Ohio, 12
Buckthorn, Common, 22, 32
Buckthorn, Glossy, 22
Bufonidae, 91
Bullfrog, American, *90*, 91
bunch grasses, 40
Burning Bush, *11*
butterflies, 110-112
Butterflyweed, 41, *41*
Butternut, 31
Buttonbush, 30, 49, *52*
Buttonbush swamp, *139*
Byron Bog, 56

c

Cactus, Eastern Prickly
   Pear, 17, *18*
Caliscelidae, 116
Canadian Heritage River
   System, 131
Carden Plain, 45
Cardinal, Northern, 12, 77-
   78, *78*
Carolinian Canada
   Coalition, 7, 122-123, 147
Carolinian Canada
   Program, 16
Carolinian Canada
   Signature Sites, 16-17
Carp, Common, 106
Carson, Peter, 142-143
Cattail, Hybrid, 59
Cecropia, 112
Chat, Yellow-breasted, 74
Chestnut blight, 31

Chestnut, American, 31
Chipmunk, Eastern, *63*, 63
Chippewa, 126, 133
Chub, Gravel, 106
Cicada, Dog-day, 113
Cicada, Scissor-grinder, 113
cicadas, 18, 39, *114*
Cicadellidae, 116-117
Clear Creek Forest, 120
Click Beetle, 39
climate change, 77, 84. *See
   also* global warming
Coffee-tree, Kentucky, 25
Colicroot, 41
Columbine, Eastern, *33*
Comma, Eastern, 110, *112*
Committee on the Status
   of Endangered Wildlife
   in Canada, 8
Committee on the Status
   of Species at Risk in
   Ontario, 8
Common Buckeye, *110*, 111
   larvae of, *110*
Compass Plant, 135
Coneflower, Gray-headed,
   42, 135, *136*
Conservation Areas,
   establishment of, 134
Conservation Authorities,
   16, 85-86, 134, 139,
   141, 147
   creation of, 138
*Conservation Authorities
   Act*, 133
Conservation Land Tax
   Incentive Program, 146
controlled burn, *37*
Coontail, 54
Cord Grass, Prairie, 40
Coreopsis, 35
COSEWIC. *See* Committee
   on the Status of
   Endangered Wildlife in
   Canada
COSSARO. *See* Committee
   on the Status of Species
   at Risk in Ontario
Cotton-grass, 56
Cottontail, Eastern, 72
Cottonwood, Swamp, 12
Cowbird, Brown-headed,
   egg of, *85*
Coyote, 62, *66*, 72, 92
Crane, Sandhill, 9
Credit River, 133
Crescent, Northern, *41*

Cricket, Snowy Tree, *115*
Cricket, Temperature. *See*
   Cricket, Snowy Tree
crickets, 113-114
Culver's-root, 35, 41

d

Dame's Rocket, 22
damselflies, 117-118
damselfly, Bluet, *117*
Dancer, Blue-ringed, 117
Dancer, Dusky, 117
Darner, Common
   Green, 118
Darner, Spadderdock, 117
Darner, Swamp, 117
Darter, Eastern Sand, *104*,
   105, 106
Darter, Greenside, 107
Darter, Least, 105
Deer, White-tailed, *71*, 72
Devonwood Conservation
   Area, *12*
Dock, Prairie, 42
Dogwood, Eastern
   Flowering, 29, 31
Dogwood, Gray, 43
Dogwood, Red-osier, 43
Dogwood, Silky, 49
Dove, Mourning, 12, 78
Doyle, Sir Arthur Conan, *47*
dragonflies, 117-118
Dropseed, Prairie, 40
duck hunting, 15
Duck, Wood, 77, 83
Dundas Valley, *32*, 86, 124
Duskywing, Persius, 111
Duskywing, Wild
   Indigo, 110
Dutch elm disease, 31
Dutchman's Breeches, *32*
Dutton Prairie, *135*, 135-136

e

Eagle, Bald, 15, *73*, 73
Eastern Massasauga
   Recovery Team, 96
Ecological Gifts
   Program, 146
Egret, Great, 10, 79
Elfin, Frosted, 111
Elk. *See* Wapiti
Elm, American, 31, 42
Emerald Ash Borer, 13
Environment Canada, 98
Environmental Farm
   Plans, 148
Erigan River, 124

Essex Region Conservation Authority, 44
European occupancy, 126-28
exotic species, invasive, 13, 22, 31, 103-104, 106

f
False Solomon's Seal, 23
Fanshawe Dam, *137*
Federation of Ontario Naturalists. *See* Ontario Nature
Fern, Broad Beech, 25
Fern, Christmas, 24
Fern, Sensitive, 24
fireflies, 115-116
Firefly, Big Dipper, 115-116
fishes, 104-107
fishing industry, 14-15
Flowering Spurge, 35
Flycatcher, Acadian, 74, 80-81, *80*, 85
Fonthill Kame, 86
Fox, Gray, 69-70, 72
Fox, Red, *64*, 69, 92
Foxsnake, Eastern, 95, *96*, *98*
Fringed Puccoon, 41
Frog, Blanchard's Cricket, 91
Frog, Northern Leopard, 91
Frog, Western Chorus, 91
frogs, 90-91

g
Gar, Spotted, 105
Gartersnake, Butler's, 94
Gartersnake, Eastern, 94
Gartshore, Mary, 142-143
Gentian, Bottle, 42
Gentian, Cream, 42
Gentian, Fringed, 42, *42*
Gentian, Prairie, *42*
Gentian, Stiff, 42
Giant Reed Grass, 54, 55, 58-59
Ginseng, American, cultivated, *132*, 133
Glider, Spot-winged, 118
global warming 58. *See also* climate change
Gnatcatcher, Blue-gray, 79
Goat's-rue, Virginia, 41
Goby, Round, 13, 94, 106
Goldenrod, Canada, 42
Goldenrod, Riddell's, 42
Goldenrod, Rigid, 42
Goldenrod, Showy, 42
Goldenrod, Tall, 42
Goose, Canada, 73, *82*, 83, 136-137
Grackle, Common, 9-10
Grama, Side-oats, 40

Grand River, 104, 108, *131*, 133
Graphocephala coccinea, 116, *116*
grasses, prairie, 40
grasshoppers, 113-114
Grass-of-Parnassus, 54, 55
Green Dragon, 25
Grosbeak, Blue, 84
Grosbeak, Rose-breasted, 75, 76-77
Gum, Black, *31*

h
Hackberry Butterfly, 110
Hairstreak, Edward's, 111
Hairstreak, Northern, 110
Haldimand Clay Plain, 56
Hamilton Conservation Authority, 32
Hamilton Naturalists' Club, 138
Hare, European, 63-64
Hawk, Red-shouldered, 79-80, *79*
Hazel, American, 43
Hedge-Parsley, 22
Hemlock, Eastern, 26, 27, 34, 129
Hepatica, 23
Heron, Great Blue, 10
herring, 15
Hibiscus, 55
Hickory, Bitternut, 30
Hickory, Pignut, 30, 42
Hickory, Shagbark, 30, 42
Hickory, Shellbark, 30
Hilts, Stewart, 140
Holiday Beach, 86
Hoptree, Common, 21, 109
horsetail, 24
Hummel, Monte, 139
Hurricane Hazel, 138
Hyacinth, Wild, 44
Hylidae, 91
hypsithermal period, 39
Hyssop, Giant Yellow, 25

i
Important Bird Area (IBA), 86
Indian Grass, 40, 136
industrialization, 130-131
insects, singing, 113-114
Ipperwash, 116-117
Iroquois, 126
Islands of Green, 140
Ivey Foundation, 141

j
Jameson, Anna, 22
Jumping Mouse, Meadow, 71

Jumping Mouse, Woodland, *72*
June Beetles, 39

k
Kalm's Brome Grass, 40
Karner Blue butterfly, 13, 37, 62, 111, *111*, 138
Karner Blue Sanctuary, 37
Katydid, Northern True, 114
katydids, 10, 113-114
Kelly, Kenneth, 133
Kestrel, American, *75*
Kirk, Malcolm, 140
Komoka, 134

l
Labrador-tea, 56
Lady Beetles, Multicoloured Asian, *120*
Lady Beetles, Seven-spotted, *120*
Lady's-slipper orchid, hybrid, *41*
Lady's-slipper, Small White, 22, 41
Lake St. Clair Marshes, *128*
Lambton County Heritage Forest, 86
Lambton Wildlife Inc., 37
Lamprey, Sea, 106
Lampyiridae, 115
landowner-contact program, 140
Larch, 12
leafhopper, *Prairiana*, 117
leafhoppers, 116-117
Leatherleaf, 56
Lily, Wood, 41
Liriodendron, 26
lizards, 93
Long Point, *14*, 15, 60, 66, 87, 120, 134
Long Point Marsh, 86
Long Point Provincial Park, 16
Long-horned Beetle, Asian, 13, 31
Longwoods Conservation Area, 126
Loosestrife, Purple, 22, 58
Lotus, American, 10, 54, *54*
Love Grass, Purple, 40
Lower Grand River Trust, 139
lumber industry, 13, 129-130
Luna moth, 20, *113*
Lupine, Wild, 37, 111
Lynx, 62, 64, 71

m
Madtom, Brindled, 107, *107*
Madtom, Northern, 100, 106

Magnolia, Cucumber, 25, *26*
magnolias, 26
Mallow, Swamp Rose, 55
mammoth, 125
Mandarin, Yellow, 25
Manitoulin Island, 45
Maple, Red, 30
Maple, Silver, 31
Maple, Sugar, 24, 26
mastodon, 125
Mayapple, 23, 29
Mayflower, Canada, 29
McGill, Larry, 145
McNiff, Patrick, 36
Meadowlark, Eastern, 84
Merganser, Hooded, *77*
Miami Mist, 44, *41*
Middle Island, 138
Milbert's Tortoiseshell, 110
Milksnake, Eastern, 95
Milkweed, Common, 41
Milkweed, Purple, *41*
Miner, Jack, 136-137
Ministry of Natural Resources, 141
Mockingbird, Northern, 12, 74, 79
Mohawk, 126
Mole, Eastern, 65, 66-67, 71
Monarch, 18, 41, *62*, 111, 118, *119*
Moneywort, 22
Moraviantown, 133
moths, 112-113
Mountain Lion, 13, 64, 71
Mountain-mint, 41
Mourning Cloak, 110-111
Mouse, House, 63-64
Mucket, 101
Mudpuppy, Common, 89, 102
Munsee-Delaware, 133
Muskellunge, 105
Muskrat, 103
Mussel, Mapleleaf, 101
Mussel, Quagga, 94
Mussel, Salamander, 100, 102
Mussel, Zebra, 13, 17, 94, 104
mussels, freshwater, 17, 100-104
Mustard, Garlic, 22, 31

n
Natural Heritage Information Centre, 8, 98, 123
Natural Heritage League, 139
Nature Conservancy of Canada, 44, 138, 140, 143, 147

Neutrals, 126
New Jersey Tea, 43
Newt, Eastern, 90
Newt, Red-spotted, 90
newts, 88-90
Niagara Escarpment, 122
Nighthawk, Common, 85
Norfolk Field
    Naturalists, 142
Norfolk Land Trust, 139
Norfolk Sand Plain, 41, 69, 70, 95
North American Butterfly Association, 120
Noss, Reed, 144

O

Oak Ridges Moraine, 144
Oak, Black, 25, 30, 42
Oak, Bur, 42
Oak, Chinquapin, 30, 42, 45
Oak, Dwarf Chinquapin, 25, 28
Oak, Pin, 25, 30, 42
Oak, Red, 30
Oak, Shumard, 25, 30
Oak, Swamp White, 30, 31
Oak, White, 30, 42
oak-hickory forest, 29-30
Ojibway Prairie Complex, 95, 109, 116, 119, 120
Ojibway Prairie Provincial Nature Reserve, 35, 35-36
Olive, Russian, 22
Onadata, 117 18
Oneida, 133
Onion, Nodding, 44, 45
Ontario Breeding Bird Atlas, 12
Ontario Farm Tile Drainage Act, 133
Ontario Heritage Foundation, 140, 141
Ontario Nature, 44, 138, 140
Opossum, Virginia, 64, 65, 65-66, 72, 92
Orchid, Eastern Prairie Fringed, 41
Otter, River, 64, 71
Ovenbird, 74, 75
Owl, Barn, 80, 80, 84
Owl, Eastern Screech, 8, 29
Owl, Short-eared, 84

P

paddlefish, 13
Painted Lady, 111
Paleo-Indians, 125
Paper Pondshell, 101
Parakeet, Carolina, 13
Pawpaw, 13, 25
peatlands, 55-56

Pelee Island, 15, 41, 44, 45, 91, 120, 140
Perch, Yellow, 104
Photinus, 116
Photuris, 115-116
Pickerel-weed, 54
Pigeon, Passenger, 13, 73
piglet bug, 116
Pigtoe, Round, 101
Pike, Blue. *See also* Blue Walleye, 106
Pimpleback, 101, 101
Pine, White, 26, 30
Pinery, 93, 119, 120, 127, 134
Pinery Provincial Park, 16, 72, 82
Pipistrelle, Eastern, 67
Pitcher Plant, 56
Plover, Piping, 15, 73-74
Point Abino, 86, 87
Point Pelee, 15, 41, 86, 89, 93, 104, 120, 134
Point Pelee Marsh, 60
Point Pelee National Park, 10, 16, 48, 72, 118
Poison Ivy, 43, 52, 57
Polyphemus, 112
Pond-lily, 54
Pope, William, 15, 20
Pottawatomie, 38
prairie,
    management of, 118 119
    woody plants of, 42-43
Prieksaitis, Bill, 135
Promethea moth, 112
    caterpillar of, 113
provincial parks, 16
Potawatami Swamp, 52
Pterophylla, 141, 142

q

Queen Snake, 94, 95
Queen Victoria Niagara Falls Park, 122
Question Mark butterfly, 111

r

Raccoon, 63, 72, 72, 92, 103
Rail, King, 80, 85
Rainy River, 37
RAMSAR Convention, 60
Ranidae, 91
Rat, Norway, 63-64
Ratsnake, Eastern, 95
Rattlesnake, Eastern Massasauga, 94, 95-96, 95
Rattlesnake, Timber, 14, 88, 95
rattlesnakes, 14
Rayed Bean, 100, 102
Recovery Strategy Group, 46
Redhorse, Golden, 105, 105

Reid, Ron, 140
Rice Lake Plains, 36
Riffleshell, Northern, 100, 100, 101, 107
Rondeau, 87, 93, 119, 134
Rondeau Provincial Park, 49, 72, 86, 122
Rose, Prairie, 42
Rouge Park, 16
Rubyspot, American, 117, 117
Rubyspot, Smoky, 117
Rue-anemone, 25

S

Saddleback moth, caterpillar of, 113
Saddlebag, Black, 118
Saddlebag, Carolina, 118
Saddlebag, Red, 118
Salamander, Allegheny Mountain Dusky, 89
Salamander, Eastern Red-backed, 88, 89
Salamander, Eastern Tiger, 88, 89, 90
Salamander, Northern Dusky, 89
Salamander, Northern Spring, 88, 89
Salamander, Spotted, 88
salamanders, 88-90
salamanders, mole. *See Ambystoma*
salmon, 13
Sargeant, Bill, 139
Sassafras, 12, 25, 113
sawmill, 129
Selkirk Provincial Park, 16
Seneca, 126
Shiner, Pugnose, 105, 106
Short Hills Nature Sanctuary, 138
Short Hills Provincial Park, 16
Shrew, Least, 65, 66
Shrew, Pygmy, 66
Shrike, Loggerhead, 74
Sifton Bog, 56, 72
Signature Sites, 140
Silkmoth, Tulip-tree, 112
Simcoe, Lady Elizabeth, 14, 57
Six Nations of the Grand River, 133, 145
Ska-Nah-Doht, 126
Skimmer, Twelve-spotted, 118
Skink, Common Five-lined, 93, 93
Skipper, Duke's, 110
Skipper, Fiery, 111
Skipper, Hoary Edge, 110

Skunk Cabbage, 30-31, 34, 34
Skunk, Striped, 92, 86, 95, 117, 120
Slider, Red-eared, 96-97
Smelt, Rainbow, 106
snakes, 93-96
Sneezeweed, 55
Snout, American, 120
Snuffbox, 101
South Walsingham forest complex, 142
South Walsingham Sand Ridges, 30, 86
Sparrow, Henslow's, 74, 84
Sparrow, Swamp, 9
Sparrow, Vesper, 84
species at risk, 8, 33, 43, 74, 84-85, 91, 92, 96, 100, 106-108
Spencer Gorge, 121, 122
Sphagnum moss, 56
Spicebush, 30, 113
Spike, 101
spike-rush marsh, 14
Spooky Hollow, 86
Spooky Hollow Sanctuary, 138, 138
Spring Beauty, 23, 29
Spring Creek, 124
Spruce, Black, 12, 56
Spruce, White, 56
Squamata, 93
Squirrel, Eastern Fox, 63-64, 64
Squirrel, Eastern Gray, 63, 67-68, 68
Squirrel, Southern Flying, 68, 68, 72
St. Clair Marsh, 60, 86
St. Clair National Wildlife Area, 104-105
St. Clair River, 133
St. John's Conservation Area, 16
St. Williams Conservation Reserve, 86
Star-grass, Water, 54
Star-grass, Yellow, 41
Stead, Ken, 142
Stephenson, Bill, 144
Stone Road Alvar, 44, 45, 138, 140
Stoneroller, Central, 107
Strawberry, Wild, 41
sturgeon, 13
Sturgeon, Lake, 105, 107
Sulphur Creek, 124
Sumac, Fragrant, 43
Sumac, Poison, 57
Sumac, Smooth, 43
Sumac, Staghorn, 43
sundew, 56

Sunfish, Longear, *106*
Sunflower, Pale-leaved, 42
Sunflower, Tall, 42
Sunflower, Thin-leaved, 42
Sunflower, Woodland, 42
Swallowtail, Eastern
 Tiger, *109*
 larva of, *111*
Swallowtail, Giant, 18, 110
Swallowtail, Zebra, 110
swamps, 52-53
Swan, Tundra, *77*, *82*, 128
Switch Grass, 40
Sycamore, American, 31, 42
Sydenham River, *99*, 100,
 104, 107-108, 117
Sydenham River Recovery
 Strategy, 108

t
Talbot Settlement, 127
Tallgrass Ontario, 46
Tamarack, 56
Tanager, Scarlet, *61*, 75,
 76, 76
Tanager, Summer, 84
Tape-grass, 54
Tern, Black, *84*, 85
Thames River, 100, 106,
 108, 117, 133
Three Awn, Arrow
 Feather, 40
Thrush, Wood, 74, 76
Tick-trefoil, Canada, 35
Tick-trefoil, Showy, 41
Titmouse, Tufted, 12, 74
Toad, American, 87
Toad, Fowler's, 17, 62, *87*, 91
toads, 90-91

Toothwort, 23, 29
Toronto Zoo, 98
tree cricket, 10
Treefrog, Gray, 10, *91*
Trillium, Red, 29
Trillium, White, 23, *23*,
 25, 29
Trout Lily, 23, 29
Trout, Brown, 104
Trumpet Creeper, 25
Tulip-tree, 12, 18, 25-26, *25*,
 34, 81, 109
Tupelo, 12, 25
Turkey Point, 15, 86, 119, 138
Turkey Point Provincial
 Park, 16
Turkey, Wild, 73, 83-84, *83*
Turtle, Blanding's, 10, *92*
Turtle, Eastern Box, 97
Turtle, Painted, 92
turtle, predated nest of, *93*
Turtle, Snapping, 92
Turtle, Spiny Softshell, *92*
Turtle, Spotted, *91*
turtles, 91-92
Twayblade, Purple, 41

u
underwing moths, 112-113
Underwing, Darling, 113
Underwing, Dejected, 113
Underwing, The
 Sweetheart, 113

v
Veery, 74
 parasitized nest of, *85*
Vetch, Wood, 41
Violet, 29

Violet, Bird's Foot, 15, 41
Vireo, Red-eyed, 75
Vireo, White-eyed, 74
Vole, Meadow, 71
Vole, Woodland, 65, 71, 68-
 69, *69*
Vulture, Black, 84
Vulture, Turkey, 78-79, *78*

W
Wahoo. *See* Burning Bush
Wainfleet Bog, 56, 95
Waldron, Gerry, 12
Walleye, 104
Walnut, Black, 13, *19*
Walpole Island, 38, 41, 42,
 86, 133
Walpole Island First
 Nation, 43, 145
Wapiti, 64, 71
War of 1812-14, 128
Warbler, Cerulean, 81
Warbler, Hooded, 18, 82
Warbler, Prothonotary, 34,
 74, *81*, 82, 85
 nest boxes for, *139*
Warbler, Worm-eating, 84
Wartyback, Purple, 101
Water Buttercup, 54
Water Smartweed, 54
Water-lily, White, 54
Watershield, 54
Watersnake, Lake Erie, 94-
 95, *94*
Watersnake, Northern, 94
Waterthrush, Louisiana,
 74, 85, *85*
Wavyrayed Lampmussel,
 100, 102-103

West Elgin Nature Club,
 135-136
West Elgin Stewardship
 Council, 136
Wetland Drain Restoration
 Project, 60
wetlands, 48-51, 53-55
 future of, 56-60
 plant communities of,
 51-52
Wheatley Provincial
 Park, 16
Whip-poor-will, 85
White Heel-splitter, 100
Wild Ginger, 23
Wild Rice, 54, *57*, 86
wildflowers, prairie, 40-42
Wildlife Habitat
 Canada, 141
Wilds of Pelee Island, 44
wine industry, 134
Witch-hazel, 29, *29*
Woodchuck, 70, *70*, 71
Woodland period, 125
Woodland Recovery
 Program, 148
Woodpecker, Pileated, 28
Woodpecker, Red-bellied,
 10, 12, 20
Wood-Pewee, Eastern, 74,
 75-76
World Biosphere
 Reserve, 122
World Wildlife Fund, 140
Wren, Carolina, 12, 10, 74

y
Yellowthroat, Common, 9

PHOTOGRAPHY CREDITS

T=top, B=bottom, M=middle, L=left, R=right

A. Dextrase, OMNR: 104; Al Woodhouse: 4, 33T, 33B, 64, 90, 117T; Ben and Brenda Kulon: 111T, 112, 113T, 120T; Brenda Kulon: 8, 75; Brock Fenton: 67; Calvin Knaggs: 88T; Don Gordon, UTRCA: 130, 137; Donald Kirk: 7, 23, 24T, 29, 32, 40, 41 second to B, 44, 45, 58, 64, 109, 124, 131, 138, 141; Duncan Gow, CWS: 77B; Gerry Clements: 110T, 110B; Ian Carmichael: 111B, 113B, 116, 117B; Jacques Giraud: 125; Jane Bowles: 14, 50, 51, 52T, 52B, 54T, 54 second to T, 54B, 59, 60, 86, 120B; Jim Flynn: back cover centre, back cover TR, back cover BL, 68B, 74B, 74T, 77T, 78T, 93B, 119; John (Sandy) Dobbyn: 61, 72T, 78B, 89, 91T, 139; John Haggeman, CWS: 128; John MacRae: 34, 42 second to B, 42 second to T, 73, 79, 82T, 95T, 114, 118; Jon Brierley: 63, 72M;

L. Lamb: back cover BM, 10, 12, 18, 22, 24B, 26, 38, 42T, 46, 48T, 48B, 108, 135, 136; Lambton Heritage Museum: 127; Mary Gartshore: 11, 30, 31, 72B, 82B, 85T, 87, 123, 142, 143; Michael Patrikeev: 65, 69, 80T, 85B, 115B; New York State Department of Environmental Conservation: 105T, 105B, 107; P.A. Woodliffe: front cover, inside front flap, back cover TL, back cover ML, back cover TL, 1, 17, 25, 35, 36, 37, 40B, 41B, 41T, 41 second to T,42B, 43, 49, 53, 54 second to B, 57, 71, 81, 84, 94, 97, 113M, 140; Paul Armstrong: 92B; Paul Pratt: 115T; Ron Gould: 70; Royal Ontario Museum: 55T, 55B, 56; Sandy Bell: back cover BR, 6, 15, 19, 20, 21, 25B, 27, 28, 32B, 47, 62, 66, 68T, 76, 80B, 83, 121, 132, 134; Scott Gillingwater: 91B, 92T, 93T, 95B, 96, 98; Shawn Staton: 99, 100, 101T, 101B, 102, 106; Todd Morris, DFO: 103; University of Western Ontario Archives: 129